Fortress • 50

The Forts of Celtic Britain

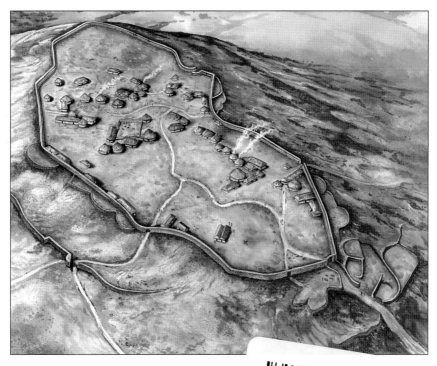

Angus Konstam · Illustrated by

Series editors Marcus Cowper and Nikolai Bogdanovic

First published in 2006 by Osprey Publishing
Midland House, West Way, Botley, Oxford OX2 0PH, UK
443 Park Avenue South, New York, NY 10016, USA
E-mail: info@ospreypublishing.com

ISBN 10: 1 84603 064 1
ISBN 13: 978 1 84603 064 2

Cartography: Map Studio, Romsey, UK
Typeset in Monotype Gill Sans and ITC Stone Serif
Design: Ken Vail Graphic Design, Cambridge, UK
Index by Alison Worthington
Originated by United Graphics, Singapore
Printed in China through Bookbuilders

06 07 08 09 10   10 9 8 7 6 5 4 3 2 1

A CIP catalogue record for this book is available from the British Library.

FOR A CATALOGUE OF ALL BOOKS PUBLISHED BY OSPREY MILITARY AND AVIATION
PLEASE CONTACT:

Osprey Direct, c/o Random House Distribution Center, 400 Hahn Road,
Westminster, MD 21157
Email: info@ospreydirect.com

Osprey Direct UK, P.O. Box 140, Wellingborough, Northants, NN8 2FA, UK
E-mail: info@ospreydirect.co.uk

www.ospreypublishing.com

Artist's note

Readers may care to note that the original paintings from which
the colour plates in this book were prepared are available for
private sale. All reproduction copyright whatsoever is retained by
the Publishers. All enquiries should be addressed to:

Peter Bull Art Studio
8 Hurstwood Road
Bredhurst
Gillingham
ME7 3JZ
United Kingdom

The Publishers regret that they can enter into no correspondence
upon this matter.

Measurements

Distances, ranges, and dimensions are mostly given in metric. To
convert these figures to Imperial values, the following conversion
formulae are provided:
1 metre (m)   1.0936 yards
1 kilometre (km)   0.6214 miles

The Fortress Study Group (FSG)

The object of the FSG is to advance the education of the public
in the study of all aspects of fortifications and their armaments,
especially works constructed to mount or resist artillery. The FSG
holds an annual conference in September over a long weekend
with visits and evening lectures, an annual tour abroad lasting
about eight days, and an annual Members' Day.
The FSG journal *FORT* is published annually, and its newsletter
Casemate is published three times a year. Membership is
international. For further details, please contact:

The Secretary, c/o 6 Lanark Place, London W9 1BS, UK

Contents

Introduction

Before beginning any discussion of 'the forts of Celtic Britain', it is important to try to define just what constituted a Celtic fort, and who the Celts actually were. We also need to know when they built the fortified structures which still dot the landscape of modern Britain – if indeed they were responsible for such structures. Archaeologists and historians are unable to define whether Britain truly was Celtic, who the Celts actually were, or whether many of their 'forts' were really designed as military enclosures. Some archaeologists even categorize the stone-built brochs of northern Scotland as cattle sheds; in truth, they are more like medieval stone keeps.

Identifying who the Celts were is something of a historical minefield, the evidence being drawn from the accounts of classical writers, the surviving archaeological remains, and traces of linguistic links which can still be found on the 'Celtic fringe' of Ireland, Wales, Cornwall, Brittany and the Scottish Highlands. Unfortunately, these three strands fail to provide all the answers, and sometimes contradict each other. The first classical references to the Celts by Greek historians occur in the 6th century BC, when the people called the 'Keltoi' were identified as occupying the lands to the north of the Greek peninsula. The Keltoi raided into Greece and Italy, and in 390 BC they even sacked Rome. The Romans subsequently paid more attention to their neighbours, particularly after the former expanded into northern Italy and the French Mediterranean coast. They described the people they encountered as the Celts (or *Galli* in Latin). Some historians, such as Posidonius (whose works were passed on by later copyists), may even have lived among the Celts while learning what he could about their culture.

In the mid-1st century BC, Julius Caesar provided a more detailed description of the Celts (or Gauls) of what is now France in his *De Bellum Gallico* (The Gallic War). He began with his now famous account of the land he conquered:

All Gaul is divided into three parts, one of which the Belgae inhabit, the Aquitani another, those who in their own language are called Celts, or in our language Gauls, the third. All these differ from each other in language, customs and laws.

Uffington Castle, Berkshire. This substantial hill-fort was constructed around 700 BC, and encompasses an area of approximately nine acres. A white horse symbol cut into the chalk hillside adjacent to the hill-fort pre-dates the fort itself, and suggests that Uffington may have served as a site of both political and religious significance. (Author's collection)

Unfortunately neither Caesar, Strabo, nor any other classical writer had much to say of the Celts who lived in Britain. Instead we have to rely on linguistic or archaeological evidence. Elements of what was once a pan-European Celtic language still survive on the 'Celtic fringe' of Europe, where Welsh, Irish and Scots Gaelic all share the same linguistic roots. It was the 18th-century Welsh scholar Edward Lhuyd who first identified this Celtic linguistic tradition, and who first established the existence of a finite Celtic culture. Indeed it was Lhuyd who resurrected the word 'Celtic', which coincided with the emerging evidence produced through the new science of archaeology.

From the mid-19th century onwards, archaeologists began to unearth artefacts that were attributed to the Celts – as defined by Lhuyd. Two sites in particular came to be associated with particular phases of Celtic cultural development: the Late Bronze Age site at Hallstatt in Austria, and the Iron Age religious site at La Tène in Switzerland, where Celtic votive offerings were recovered from the waters of Lake Neufchâtel. Subsequently both sites gave their name to cultural phases into which all material evidence attributed to the Celts was placed. However, this was not the whole story. As evidence of the earlier Hallstatt phase can be found in some parts of Europe and not in others, archaeologists presumed that the Celtic sphere of influence expanded during the Iron Age to cover all of France, Spain, Britain, Ireland, Switzerland, Austria and parts of Italy and a swathe of Eastern European countries traversed by the River Danube. However, recent archaeological evidence has shown that even during the Late Bronze Age the indigenous (and presumably non-Celtic) peoples of Britain maintained cultural and commercial links with the Celtic peoples on the European mainland. While artefacts help explain links between different regions in the Celtic world, they do little to help us understand how the indigenous population of Britain interacted with the Celtic incomers from the Late Bronze Age onwards. In other words, the division between the Celts and those that came before them is somewhat blurred. The only clear archaeological evidence we can find is the remains of pre-Celtic and post-Celtic settlements, religious centres and defensive works.

While in recent years archaeologists and historians have become more hesitant in defining exactly who or what the Celts were, there is at least some agreement on when they lived in Britain. The Celts were essentially an Iron Age culture, a term first devised by Danish antiquarians to help them catalogue their museum collections. Today the British Iron Age is used as shorthand for the period from around 700 BC (when the production of iron first took place in Britain) until just after the Roman invasion of southern England in AD 43. Even these parameters are far from fixed: for example, it is generally held that in Scotland, where the

The earthen rampart of Uffington Castle. Archaeological evidence has shown that when it was first built the ditch was three metres deeper than it is today. (Author's collection)

While the basic shape of Uffington Castle's defensive line is pentagonal, the ditch and rampart curve in places to take advantage of minor changes in the contours. When first built the rampart would have been topped by a simple wooden palisade. (Author's collection)

Roman penetration was limited, the Iron Age continued until the 5th century AD. For the purposes of this book we will limit the study of Celtic fortifications to an even briefer period – from around 500 BC until a few decades after the first Roman invasion of Britain, c. AD 80, when most of mainland Britain had fallen under Roman control. While the Celtic period continued much later in Scotland, Wales and Ireland, the nature of 'Dark Age' Celtic fortifications is a subject worthy of another study, and will therefore remain outside the boundaries of this book. Similarly, the author has avoided coverage of Ireland, a land with its own Celtic tale to tell, which is once again deserving of its own book.

No part of the surviving physical remains of Iron Age Celtic Britain is more spectacular that the fortifications that still dot the British landscape, from the great earthen hill-forts of southern England (such as Maiden Castle) to the imposing stone-built brochs of northern Scotland. While none of these were strong enough to keep out a determined attack by the Roman war machine, they still dominated the landscape, and to the pre-Roman people of Celtic Britain they would have represented the ultimate statement in political, military and social power. This book will provide a brief survey of the types of fortifications used, and will show how they developed over time and how they changed from region to region. It is also hoped that, in some way, it will explain how these great fortifications were defended, in their role as the last bastions of Celtic civilization in Britain.

Chronology

Note: all the dates provided below for the general phases of archaeological periods are open to interpretation. They represent the broad consensus of archaeologists and historians.

2100 BC   Early Bronze Age begins.

2000 BC   The first hilltop enclosures are built in Britain.

1750 BC   Middle Bronze Age begins.

1323 BC   Death of King Tutankhamen in Egypt.

1000 BC   Late Bronze Age period begins.

800 BC   Widespread production of 'beaker' pottery in Britain.

700 BC   Early Iron Age period begins. Development of Celtic Hallstatt culture in Austria.

600 BC   Culture known as 'Iron Age A' arrives in Britain. Widespread building of hill-forts throughout Britain. Flourishing of culture in Ancient Greece.

500 BC   Middle Iron Age period. Culture known as 'Iron Age B' arrives in Britain. Celtic immigration into Britain – general growth of British population.

400 BC   Date associated with the first spread of brochs in northern Scotland. First appearance of Celtic La Tène artefacts in Britain.

200 BC   Date regarded as representing the high point of Celtic culture in Europe.

150 BC   Culture known as 'Iron Age C' arrives in Britain. Rise of large tribal kingdoms in Britain; period of warfare and general unrest. Many hill-fort defences are extensively improved.

100 BC   Late Iron Age period. First wheel-made pottery produced in Britain.

60 BC   Julius Caesar begins his ten-year conquest of Gaul. Migration of the Belgic people (Belgae) to Britain.

AD 43   The Roman invasion of Britain – the beginning of the Roman occupation.

AD 47   Roman rule consolidated south of the rivers Trent and Severn.

AD 49   Roman invasion of Wales.

AD 60   Date by which most hill-forts in southern Britain are abandoned.

AD 82   The Roman invasion of Scotland.

AD 122   Building of Hadrian's Wall.

AD 410   End of the Roman occupation of Britain. Beginning of the period known as 'Sub-Roman Britain'.

AD 500   End of the Iron Age in Scotland. Generally accepted date for the beginning of the Early Historic Period.

The western gateway at Uffington Castle is simpler than in many hill-forts, although its nature has been altered in the last two centuries. A ramp (seen in the foreground) crosses the ditch, leading to a second smaller rampart and ditch structure located where the figures are standing. (Author's collection)

Types of fortified sites

Although hill-forts and brochs are the most commonly found type of Celtic fortification in Britain, other types of fortified sites existed in tandem with them. The scope of this book precludes a study of the less defensible of these, such as lake villages and crannogs, largely because these structures lacked any obvious means of defence save their encirclement by water. Although the lake village at Glastonbury, Somerset was surrounded by a wooden palisade, it was probably not designed to keep intruders out but rather as a protective barrier to prevent children and animals falling into the surrounding lake. Similarly while buildings built over the water, such as Oakbank Crannog in Scotland's Loch Tay, may well have been defensible for a short time, it lacked the protection to keep determined attackers at bay. For the purposes of this study we shall concentrate on the Celtic sites that appear to have been designed with defence in mind.

Celtic fortifications come in a variety of types, although with the possible exception of brochs they all share certain characteristics. Over the years archaeologists have developed terminology that helps them classify the intricate systems of ditches and banks they encounter. These are often augmented with more widely understood fortification terms to help explain how these features were supposed to work. For example, many archaeologists use the words 'bank' and 'rampart' interchangeably, but to be more accurate the fortification term 'rampart' should really only be applied to the innermost bank surrounding the fort's enclosure. If a fort is enclosed by a single circuit of bank and ditch, it is described as a 'univallate' fort. More complex fortifications are described as 'bivallate' (if they have two such lines of defence), 'trivallate' (if they have three circuits of bank and ditch), and 'multivallate' (if the fort is defended by more than three lines of defence). If the banks are set close together they are described as 'compact', while the opposite are regarded as 'dispersed'.

Given the range of different types of fortifications, most fall into four general categories. The first are the pure hill-forts, whose defences are placed to make best use of the terrain. The perimeter of the enclosure follows the contours of the hilltop on which the fort is built, and consequently these fortifications are rarely circular or even regular. Instead the lines bend in accordance with the shape of the hill. The result is an irregularly shaped defensive position, but one that makes best possible use of the lie of the land. A variation on this is the headland or promontory forts found on rocky spurs of coastline where the site could be made defensible with relatively little work. In sites such as Burghead in Moray, Scotland, or Rame Head in Cornwall these fortifications close off the landward side of a headland by means of a defensive bank and ditch system similar to that found in hill-forts. The only difference is that on the remaining sides of the defended position the sea itself provides a natural barrier to attackers. It is worth noting that forts of this kind are not always found on the coast. On rare occasions where the terrain provides a similar

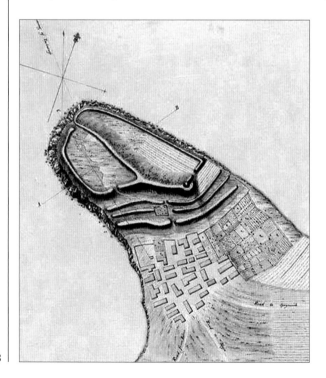

This map of the promontory fort at Burghead, Moray was drawn up by the 18th-century military surveyor General William Roy. Although the fort was associated with the Picts, it was almost certainly built earlier, during the Late Iron Age. Much of the fort was destroyed during the expansion of the town soon after Roy produced his drawing. (Society of Antiquaries, London)

advantage far from the sea, such as at the confluence of two large rivers, a similar position could also be established. An example of this is the Iron Age settlement at Dyke Hills in Oxfordshire, where the River Thame meets the River Thames near modern-day Dorchester-on-Thames. There a bivallate defensive line was created to protect the settlement, while the two rivers protected the remaining three sides of the site.

A variant on the hill-fort is what has unsatisfactorily been described as the plateau fort, or valley fort. These are similar to the more common hill-forts, but were built on sites that possessed no defensive advantages such as slopes or even rivers. Instead they had to rely on their own man-made defences to keep attackers at bay. The only real advantage of this type of fortification seems to be that in many cases the enclosure included a natural spring, so that, unlike many hill-forts, the defenders had access to water and thus in theory could better withstand a siege. Often these appear to have been built in areas of good farmland, in valleys or on broad ridges where no more obviously defensible feature was available. An example of this type of early Iron Age fort is Rainsborough in Northamptonshire, which was excavated during the 1960s. There the fortification stood on the edge of a plateau, where the ground then fell away gently into the Cherwell Valley below. It enclosed an area of some 2.5 hectares, and although its defences were univallate, the archaeologists uncovered traces of an outer bank that had been filled in at some stage during the fort's occupation. The occupants may have come to regret the siting of their fort: archaeologists also uncovered evidence that the gateway had been destroyed by fire, and a skeleton was found amid the burned ruins of a guardhouse. The inference is of course that the fort was attacked and captured probably at some point in the 3rd century BC.

Another distinct group of forts comprises those that were clearly built as non-defensible enclosures, probably to house livestock or to provide a seasonal home for a farming community. Sites of this kind were often built on the sides of a hill or in a flat area, and often involved multiple enclosures encircling a central area. While not primarily designed as a defensive position, these could serve as an emergency refuge in time of danger. Examples of forts of this type include Lordenshaws in Northumberland and Clovelly Dykes in Devon, and they are generally located in either the north of England, the south-west, or in the western

The Iron Age hill-fort at Woden Law in the Scottish Borders was built in three phases, and in its final form consisted of a double rampart and ditch. The curving double bank in the foreground has been identified as a Roman siegework, suggesting that the small hill-fort might have been besieged during Agricola's campaign in southern Scotland around AD 80–81. (RCAHMS)

The areas of major distribution of hill-forts in Britain. The main sites mentioned in the text are also indicated.

Hill-forts
Major areas of hill-fort concentration

0   50 miles
0   100km

N

SCOTLAND

Burghead
Craig Phadraig
Tap O'Noth
White Caterthun   Brown Caterthun
Barry Hill
Dunsinane
Dunadd
Dunbarton
Dun Eiden   Traprain Law
(Edinburgh Castle)   Dunsapie
Woden Law
Eildon Hill North
Lordenshaws
Burnswark

NORTH SEA

Stanwick

IRELAND

IRISH SEA

Almondbury

Caer-y-Twy
Foel Fenlli
Dinorben
Tre'r Ceiri   Dinas Emrys
Old Oswestry

Pen Dinas

WALES   ENGLAND

Caer Caradoc
Croft Ambrey

Wandlebury

Bredon Hill
Rainsborough
Ivinghoe Beacon
Uffington

Worlebury
Beacon Hill
Bratton Camp   Ladle Hill
Danebury
South Cadbury   Yarnbury   Old Winchester Hill
Blackbury Camp   St Catherine's Hill
Hambledon Hill   Old Sarum   Bury Hill
Castle Dore   Winklebury
Maiden Castle   Hod Hill   Cissbury

ENGLISH CHANNEL   FRANCE

The major areas of broch concentration in Scotland; the sites mentioned in the text are also indicated by name.

Brochs

Major areas of broch concentration

0   50 miles
0   100km

N

ATLANTIC OCEAN

Shetland Islands

Clickhimin

Mousa

Old Scatness   Jarlshof

Midhowe

Gurness

Howe

Orkney Islands

Crosskirk

Dun Carloway

Dun Dornaigil

Carn Laith

NORTH SEA

Dun Beag

Dun Vulan

Dun Telve

SCOTLAND

Dun Mor Vaul

Tirefour

Torwood

Antonine Wall

Edin's Hall

Torwoodlee

IRELAND

The Iron Age hill-fort on Barry Hill, Angus on the edge of the Scottish Highlands was built over two phases: the large oval bank of rubble that represents the later phase was built on top of an earlier earthwork. A lesser outwork protected the southern and eastern approaches to the fort, while a small area on the north side may have served as an animal enclosure. (RCAHMS)

coastal fringe of Wales. Clovelly Dykes is a prime example, with a central compound of 1.2 hectares surrounded by an oval bank and ditch, which in turn was ringed by another full bank and ditch, then two more low-banked enclosures, some of which had associated ditches in front of them. The site also boasted a large annex enclosure on its western side, protected by another ditch. In all the fortification encompassed an area of some 9.6 hectares. This complex site was expanded during its period of occupancy, as it seems the outer enclosures were added after the innermost enclosure was built. Given the minor nature of the outer works it is probable that these served as livestock enclosures, while the inner enclosure housed a small farming community or even a large farmstead.

Even smaller fortified enclosures have been found, particularly in Scotland where these structures are known as ring forts or raths. These small enclosures were almost always univallate, protected by a circular or near-circular bank and ditch system. In some cases the enclosure encompassed a natural or artificial mound, but they could also be built on level ground, such as the ring forts found in Glen Lyon, which may have been built as boundary markers or outposts, guarding the developed Iron Age community of Loch Tay and the summer pastures in the hills between the glen and the loch. Other ring works seem to have served to protect farmhouses, a little like the fortified farmhouses found in medieval Europe. Examples of these include Dan-y-Coed and Woodside, both in Dyfed, Wales. What is unusual about these last two sites is that they were strongly fortified, with a bivallate defensive system, and both were approached along a pathway lined by more banks. It has been suggested that this banked approach served as a means of herding cattle to and from the main enclosure. The impression that these were farming settlements rather than villages is enhanced by archaeological evidence of roundhouses lacking central hearths – suggesting the presence of farm buildings rather than dwelling houses.

Finally there are the brochs, the majestic stone towers found in northern Scotland. There may well have been a crossover between these buildings and the stone-clad ring forts of central Scotland or the stone-built hill-forts found in Wales. However, there is virtually no evidence that the people who built these structures had any association with the builders of Celtic sites in the rest of Britain. Given the limited scope of this book we can only touch on their basic features and suggest how they might have served the people who built them. Armit (2003) covers the subject in considerable detail, and is thoroughly recommended for those who want to explore this topic further.

Location

The hill-forts of Celtic Britain, the large earth-built structures that can be found throughout the land, are mostly concentrated in two broad areas. The first of these areas forms an elongated triangle running from the island of Anglesey in Wales southwards through the rest of Wales, beyond the Welsh mountains, then across the River Severn into modern-day England. From there the swathe runs southwards to the south Devon coast, and south-east and east to the headwaters of the River Thames, continuing to the Kentish shore. The second large band of hill-forts runs through the eastern lowlands of Scotland, from the Beauly Firth near Inverness round the coast to Aberdeen, then south through Angus and Fife to the Lothians. From there it then runs in a south-easterly direction towards the Solway Firth, which marks the English border. Hill-forts did exist outside these areas, but not in such great numbers. Within these general bands the size and style of the forts varied considerably. In very broad terms the forts found in Wales, Scotland and the north of England tend to be smaller and more numerous than the hill-forts found in the south of England. There are of course exceptions: Traprain Law and Tre'r Ceiri were as impressively large as many found further south.

These fortifications were built over a span of several centuries, and not all remained in continuous occupation throughout the Iron Age. The fact that certain areas of mainland Britain seem almost devoid of hill-forts while others have a profusion has never been fully explained, but may well represent some form of social difference between the inhabitants. Some archaeologists have argued that many of these forts represent territorial divisions, where the forts represent political statements of land ownership and boundaries as much as fortifications in their own right – akin to the feudal castles of the medieval period. Certainly some of these forts might well have served as political centres of power; the proximity of many to later Roman provincial centres is often used to support this argument. Unfortunately we know all too little about the distribution and political organization of Britain's Iron Age population, so the territorial importance of hill-forts remains a matter of speculation.

The stone-built brochs are concentrated in the north of Scotland, particularly in the northern isles of Orkney and Shetland, and the Western Isles. However, isolated examples can also be found as far south as the Scottish Borders. Their construction is unique: the largest surviving structures look more like giant kilns than fortifications. As noted previously, they also resemble the stone-built keeps built in the century after the Norman Conquest of England. Due to limitations of space, any description of these two fortification types has to remain fairly general; however, each needs to be dealt with separately as, in all but their purpose, hill-forts and brochs have little or nothing in common. A related form of Iron Age fortification is the 'dun', which in essence represents a smaller version of a broch – more like a small stone enclosure than a tower. While these may have been used as nothing more than fortified houses or farm complexes, some may well have served as important fortified sites in their own right.

The vitrified hill-fort of Mither Tap on top of Bennachie, Grampian is one of the most spectacular locations for an Iron Age fort in Scotland. The upper slopes of the mountain were encircled by a stone rampart, while traces of an inner defensive ring can also be seen. It is considered likely that the Battle of Mons Graupius between Agricola's Romans and the Caledonii in AD 84 was fought close to the foot of the mountain. (Stratford Archive)

Design and construction

Today, Celtic fortifications, particularly hill-forts, are readily identifiable by the remains of their ramparts and ditches – a still formidable system of fieldworks which serve as visible reminders of an Iron Age past in Britain. The fact that they can still be seen is a testimony to the skill with which these fortifications were sited and built, and to the longevity of the materials their builders used. These forts were built using stone, earth and timber, and all but the last of these materials have weathered the centuries. Although the era was known as the Iron Age, very little ferrous material was used in fort construction – the exception being the odd gate hinge or bracket. Similarly mortar was a post-Roman building material, and the Celts of Britain used dry-stone construction techniques in their fortifications. This was not necessarily a drawback. The fact that the Broch of Mousa in Shetland is still standing after two millennia proves that these structures were built to last.

Hill-forts: form and function

The term hill-fort is defined as a fortified enclosure, designed to take advantage of a hill or rise for its defensive advantage. The fortification could consist of one or more circular or part-circular earthen or even stone ramparts, built to follow the contours of the hill the fort was sited on. In many cases these ramparts are often associated with attendant external ditches. The structures date from the Late Bronze Age and the Iron Age.

Beyond this rather general definition, the variation in types and size of hill-forts is considerable, as are the dates given by archaeologists for the occupation. These fortifications varied from what amounted to little more than a small cattle enclosure to a fort big enough to accommodate a reasonably sized town. The larger settlement hill-forts – the type Julius Caesar called *oppida* when he encountered them in Gaul – were clearly of great importance to the people who built them, and functioned as much as a statement of regional power as a place of refuge in time of conflict. Few British sites matched the scale of these Gallic forts, although hill-forts like Maiden Castle came close. Some hill-forts functioned as permanent settlements whilst others appear only to have been occupied in time of danger, during a particular season, or for some special event. Some show little or no evidence of military use, and should therefore be seen more as enclosures to pen in domestic animals rather than as fortified strong points. The only broad definition of use is that the hill-forts were built to protect settlements or livestock from attack.

Inevitably there is some debate over how and why these hill-forts were used, and when. Most appear to have been used for at least temporary habitation or as fortified military encampments during the three centuries before the Roman conquest of Britain, which constitute the Middle and Late Iron Age, and all but a few fell into disuse after the Roman occupation. However, a few were re-occupied in the 5th century AD after the Romans left, and a few were even used as field fortifications by the Anglo-Saxons during the Viking incursions three centuries later. In areas such as northern Scotland and Wales, where the Roman influence was less pronounced, hill-forts tended to remain in use for longer.

Inevitably these multiple periods of occupation and different types of use have tended to mask the real purpose behind these fortified enclosures, and to encourage vigorous exchanges between

The small hill-fort of Caburn, Sussex was built during the early Iron Age, although archaeologists now believe its defences were strengthened around the mid-1st century AD, possibly in response to the Roman invasion of Britain. The site was abandoned soon afterwards. (Courtesy of Steve Danes)

archaeologists. The easiest way to approach this difficult subject is by expanding this broad definition of the archetypal hill-fort, showing how it might have functioned, and then looking at specific examples to see how the hill-fort changed over time, and how different fortified sites were used in different ways.

Looking at a hill-fort from outside its perimeter it is easy to forget that its most important feature was not the serried ranks of banks and ditches protecting its circumference, but the area inside the earthworks that it was supposed to protect. In the case of the majority of hill-forts the archaeological evidence of what once stood in a fort's interior is slight – at best the traces of a few earthen tracks, semi-permanent timber huts, stone-clad wells or refuse pits. Most of these features are only visible through archaeological excavation, and most hill-fort digs have revealed the shadowy traces of these signs of habitation, suggesting that the majority of hill-forts served as dwelling sites – whether designed as permanent settlements or as temporary refuges. While most sites in southern England were built on relatively low-lying hills, others in Scotland and Wales were probably too high up to remain in use throughout the year. In these cases these higher hill-forts were probably used during the summer, when livestock was moved to hillside pastures.

At Caburn, Sussex there is evidence that a second rampart and a broad but shallow ditch were added to the earlier defensive works in response to the Roman threat. Traces of both phases of construction can be seen here. (Courtesy of Steve Danes)

Hill-forts were clearly built to serve a local agrarian community rather than a military garrison, and so they were almost always located where good farmland was within easy reach. The people who built them were farmers rather than merchants or traders, and while there is archaeological evidence of metalworking and other industry, we can find little archaeological or historical evidence of hill-forts serving as trading centres or even the sites of travelling 'fairs'. All the evidence we have comes from the presence of ceramic or metal artefacts whose place of origin lay far beyond the boundaries of the community that built the fort in which the objects were found. Similarly we can only guess at the administrative or regional importance of most hill-forts, as the dearth of written evidence precludes anything more than speculation.

Building the hill-forts

Although archaeology can rarely tell us exactly why a hill-fort was built in a particular location, or even who built it, it can usually reveal something of the way the fort was built, and how it developed over time. In addition we can draw on other archaeological evidence to improve our understanding of the people

The hill-fort at Caburn, Sussex had only one entrance, sited on its north-eastern face. Archaeologists believe the mid-1st-century AD gateway consisted of a four-post box housing a recessed gate. The rampart itself was lined by a substantial palisade consisting of wooden posts set a foot apart, laced with horizontal braces and filled with chalk rubble. (Courtesy of Steve Danes)

The well-sited hill-fort on Beacon Hill, Hampshire enclosed an area of approximately 3.6 hectares. It was protected by a bank, a ditch and a counterscarp bank – pictured here as a path that now encircles the site. The traces of 20 roundhouses have been detected on its plateau-like enclosure. (Courtesy of Marcus Cowper)

who inhabited Britain during the Late Bronze Age and the Iron Age, and to show what tools and techniques they could apply to a major building project such as this.

The site of the fort seemed to be crucial. In some places hill-forts were built within sight of each other, which has led to the theory that they constituted an interconnected network of defences – akin to an Iron Age Maginot Line. While this notion has largely been discredited, it does appear that forts were built to dominate the immediate hinterland, usually on a hill overlooking an arable and populous valley. Whatever the reason for construction, these Iron Age 'engineers' certainly knew how to take advantage of the terrain. Almost without exception British Celtic hill-forts were sited to make the best possible use of the contours of the hill on which they were built. In other words the steepness of the slope on one or more sides of the position, the proximity of rivers and streams, or the visibility of any approaching force were all factors used to decide where the fort should be built.

The following account of the building process is gleaned from the archaeological investigation of Ladle Hill fort, Hampshire, which was excavated by Professor Piggott in 1931. What was unusual about the site was that it was never completed, and so traces of several phases of building could be identified. About a third of the 3.3-hectare (8-acre) site was already delineated by an existing boundary ditch before the construction work began, and this feature was utilized by the builders to help them. The rest of the circumference was delineated by a series of ditches, where the excavated earth was piled into mounds on the inner side of the ditch. Piggott detected the hand of at least 12 digging teams at work, but the project ended before the various teams could link their ditches together. In effect, Ladle Hill is a perfect example of an Iron Age building site.

The first stage must have been to mark out the near-circular course of the ditch. We know enough about Celtic society to imagine that some form of druidic religious ceremony would have been involved. In at least one hill-fort the remains of what might have been a sacrificial victim have been found, suggesting that the British Celts took the idea of honouring a deity very seriously. However, all our direct accounts of druidic practices come from non-Celtic or post-Roman Celtic sources, and the exact nature of these ceremonies is very much a matter of speculation. After the ceremonies came the hard labour – digging the ditch. As already noted, several teams began work at the same time in different parts of the perimeter. At Ladle Hill this first ditch was never completed, but the sections that were dug were of a fairly uniform size, approximately 1.5m deep and 3m wide.

Rather than simply dumping the soil on the inner face of the ditch to form the rampart, the teams carried their soil a few yards inside the fort, creating a series of temporary soil dumps. This allowed the walls to be built with some care: a base and inner revetment of large chalk boulders was created, and the rest of the soil was used as infill. A timber framework would have been constructed – essentially a wooden cage within which the rubble and soil would have been poured. The slope on the outer side of the bank would have been more substantial than on the inner face, so a stone or timber revetment would have been essential to keep the soil in place. This inner revetment was substantial, as it was also designed to reinforce the bank and prevent it from collapsing. This was not an easy task, given the simple tools available, and the construction of a revetment of this kind represented a feat of engineering that belied the idea that the builders lacked engineering skills. Amazingly, in sites where evidence of this timber framework has survived, there is no sign that nails were used; the structure was either slotted together, or tied into place. It also involved a lot of work. Evidently the idea of carrying the same load of soil twice was clearly considered a necessary sacrifice in order that the finished wall could be built in a methodical manner. At Ladle Hill the eastern portion of the rampart was built to what must have been its full planned height of around four metres, with a substantial chalk revetment bracing it. The bank was approximately seven metres wide, tapering on its outside face to a narrower platform of approximately one metre. A similar smaller section of rampart was completed on the fort's western side, but the two sections remained unconnected. It is almost as if the number of skilled wall-builders was smaller than the number of men required to dig and transport the soil – which was almost certainly the case. This suggests the presence of experienced supervisors.

The hill-fort of St. Catherine's Hill, Hampshire was excavated in the late 1920s, the first scientific hill-fort excavation in Britain. The oval perimeter encloses a gently sloping hilltop area of nine hectares. This main gateway shows signs of being hastily re-fortified, the builders creating an elaborate defensive system incorporating a chalk-walled approach and guardhouses. The hill-fort shows signs of being stormed in the mid-1st century AD, presumably by the Romans. (Courtesy of Marcus Cowper)

Ladle Hill is not the only fort where the work remained unfinished. In several other cases improvements to existing fortifications show signs of having never been completed, particularly in the south of England. As many of these features have been dated to around the mid-1st century AD, these may well have represented emergency construction programmes begun as a response to the Roman invasion of Britain. The fact that they were unfinished may be explained by either the speed of the Roman advance through the region, or by the diversion of the labour force into mobile armies, charged with contesting the invasion. It is interesting that in most of these cases the work also appears to have been undertaken by several teams working simultaneously. The time taken to build a fort in this manner would obviously depend upon the size and availability of the workforce, or the size of a perceived threat to the community that undertook the work. In the case of larger hill-forts such as Maiden Castle construction of the perimeter defences could well have taken several years, particularly as the workforce almost certainly had to fit the work in between the seasonal demands imposed by arable farming during the Iron Age.

Once the rampart and ditch had been completed, the fort-builders would begin work on the palisade, which would surmount the bank. In most cases this involved the sinking of a line of timber posts about one metre apart around the outer edge of the rampart, then linking these with cross-braces. The structure would then be completed by filling the gaps between the posts with large stakes, thereby creating a solid palisade. We shall look into the nature of these timber defences in more detail, but at Ladle Hill the wooden perimeter would have been completed by the building of one or more gateways. As the fort was never finished and its perimeter never completely dug, we cannot be sure how many gates were planned to be incorporated into the Ladle Hill defences. However, if we look at the evidence from other forts such as Danebury in Hampshire we can imagine how these would have looked. Stout posts would have been dug between two inwardly turning spurs of rampart, and the palisade would have run up to these gateposts. For easier opening the wooden gate would have been built in two parts; these were secured to the posts using iron fittings.

The completed structure would have involved a substantial ditch – no doubt deeper and possibly wider than the preliminary ditch that was dug before work stopped on the site. In forts of similar size the ditch could be up to three or four metres deep. From there a steep glacis would rise up seven metres towards a wooden palisade, supported and braced using stout timber posts and beams. A narrow wall-walk behind the palisade would have provided a fighting platform, and from there the bank would have fallen sharply away towards the interior of the fort. A stone revetment would have prevented this bank from being eroded through use. We cannot tell if a more elaborate structure was planned at Ladle

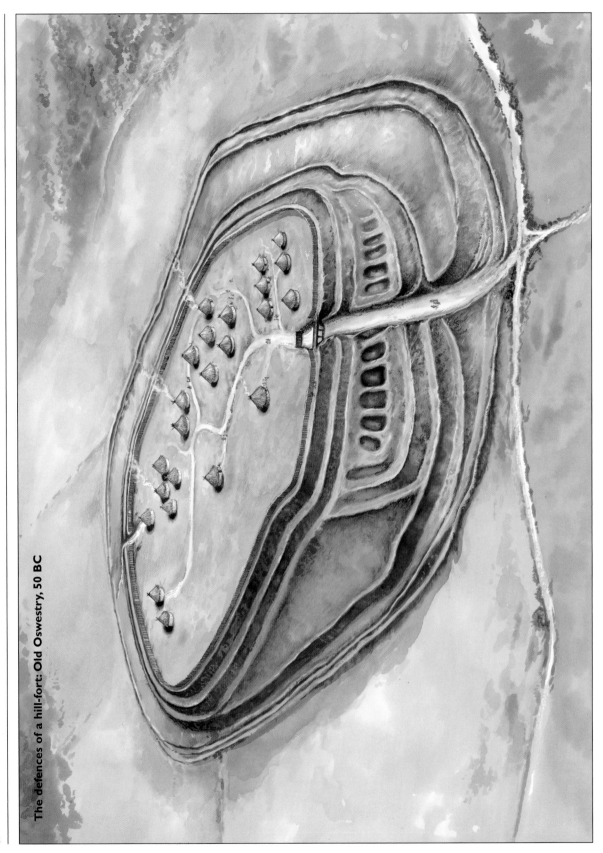

The defences of a hill-fort: Old Oswestry, 50 BC

The defences of a hill-fort: Old Oswestry, 50 BC
This impressive hill-fort encloses an area of 5.3 hectares (13 acres), and was the subject of an excavation during the late 1930s. It appears the fort was built in three phases from around 600 BC until the arrival of the Romans in the mid-1st century AD. During each phase an additional bank and ditch was added to the structure, although the final (outermost) phase of construction undertaken around 150 BC was by far the most extensive. During this last phase the gatehouse was strengthened with the addition of a series of banked enclosures or annexes on either side of it. Most probably these served as miniature fortified positions from which the defenders could fire upon any attacker who attempted to reach the gateway via the walkway bridge. Like most hill-forts, the principal line of defence was the innermost bank or rampart – the outer banks and ditches would have served to slow down an attacker, or even to keep him beyond slingshot range of the inner defences. The weak point of any hill-fort was its wooden gateway, so this was where the defenders concentrated their efforts, developing 'killing grounds' which covered all approaches to the vulnerable gateway.

Hill, where defensive works outside the gateway or additional counterscarp ditches would have been added. What we can calculate is the time taken for the builders to complete the structure they began work on.

Had it been completed, the hill-fort at Ladle Hill would have involved the transportation of some 11,000m³ of soil, boulder and rubble dug from the ditch; in addition, if suitable stones could not be found these would have had to be moved to the site from elsewhere. Once the material from the ditch had been graded and sorted it would have had to be moved again, this time to the site of the rampart. If we apply the construction yardstick where a man can dig and transport one cubic metre of soil per day (given the simple tools available), and assuming that half as much time again would be needed for the subsequent re-transportation of the soil at the rampart site, this means the digging and soil moving alone would have taken around 16,500 man days of work. Included in this total is the time taken to build the revetment. Given the perimeter of the bank would have been about 680m long, we can assume the builders would have needed about 1,000 small trees to provide the posts, braces and stakes needed to build the palisade and gateway. We can add another 500 man days for this work, giving a rough total of 17,000 man days. Archaeologists have determined that for each hectare enclosed within a fort the defences could house and protect approximately 60 people. That gives us a workforce of 200, a total that would include women and children (who would have been used to transport the soil in baskets). If we reduce the workforce by a quarter to include the lesser contribution of the elderly and the children, we are left with a total project time of approximately 112 days, or roughly four months.

The hill-fort on Beacon Hill, Hampshire was served by only one entrance sited on its south-western face, consisting of bank and rampart that turned back on itself to house a simple gate. This entrance was mirrored by a similar feature on the counterscarp bank, while the entrance was further protected by an additional smaller semi-circular bank and ditch beyond the counterscarp. (Courtesy of Marcus Cowper)

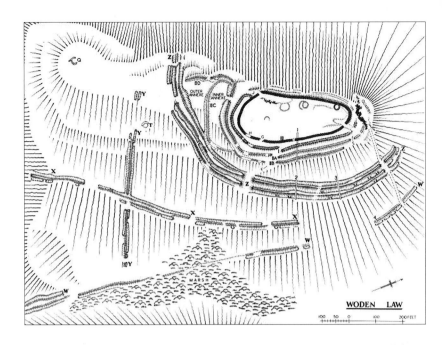

The same equation can be extended to include other similar hill-forts, including Maiden Castle. The only difference would have been that in several of these sites the defences were built in several phases, often a century or more apart. These earlier works were often incorporated into the new design, which reduced the amount of work involved. However, in its final phase Maiden Castle was protected by no fewer than three banks and a counterscarp bank, and three ditches. In addition the gatehouse defences were significantly grander than those that would have been built at Ladle Hill. The hill-fort historian A.H.A. Hogg estimated that in time of peace the defences of Maiden Castle could have been improved from one building phase to another in a period of approximately five to seven months. As this would have involved an unacceptable degree of disruption to the farming life of the community, he argues that the work would have been spread out over two or even three seasons. In many ways Ladle Castle was the ideal size – a smaller hill-fort would almost certainly have served a smaller population, which meant the work involved would have taken longer. Here again the work would have imposed on the agrarian calendar, and so would probably have been undertaken over at least two years.

The design of brochs

Unlike the hill-forts found elsewhere in Britain, the brochs of northern Scotland were defensive works designed to protect a relatively small number of people. The term 'broch' is generally used to refer to a free-standing, round, stone-built tower, although several of these may also have been built as a centrepiece of a fortified settlement. Their origins remain something of a mystery. One early theory was that they were built by an influx of newcomers – refugees from the Roman invasion of Britain. However, since no similar structures existed further south, this notion is easy to disprove. Also, most brochs have been dated to between 500 and 200 BC, although they remained in continuous use until the Roman period. The best-surviving broch structure at Mousa in Shetland was built around AD 100, and remained in use for approximately two centuries. The dates apply to other sites too, as at some date after AD 100 the majority of brochs appear to have fallen into disrepair. In structures such as the Broch of Gurness, where the tower was surrounded by a fortified settlement, the village itself seems to have been abandoned, and the stone re-used to construct farm buildings close to the old site.

The communities served by these fortifications must have been small compared to the Iron Age communities who built hill-forts, but then the two types of fortification do not bear close comparison. Given the correlation between hill-fort size and the estimated number of people who lived in or beneath it, only the smallest hill-forts can be compared in scale to these brochs. Both involved a considerable amount of effort for the small agrarian community who built them, particularly when some hill-forts or brochs seem to have been little more than fortified farms, serving at most one or two extended families. It has therefore been suggested that in places like Orkney or Shetland, where these broch structures are common, neighbouring communities pooled their efforts and helped out in the construction of each other's tower – similar to the communal barn-building tradition of the Amish community in the United States.

Eildon Hill North, Roxburgh is one of three hills dubbed 'Trimontium' by the Romans, and the site of Scotland's largest hill-fort, enclosing an area of some 16 hectares. It was thought to be the main stronghold of the Selgovae before it was captured by the Romans in AD 80, although recently archaeologists have called this assumption into question. (Historic Scotland)

A typical broch was built using dry-stone walling, and was approximately 20m in diameter. The broch at Mousa stands some 13m high, although others might well have been lower structures – no more than five metres in height. The walls were double-skinned, with a cavity between them wide enough to fit a staircase that wound its way up to the top of the tower. In most large brochs the walls are approximately three metres thick. The structure was entered through a small, low doorway; these were often flanked by guard chambers to improve the security of the fortification. The interior was almost certainly divided into floors, each level being accessed from the stairway and its attendant galleries. In brochs such as Gurness, Midhowe and Mousa the lower floor contained a stone-lined well and food storage pits, which meant the defenders could withstand a lengthy siege. Archaeological evidence suggests that the whole structure was capped by a conical pitched roof of thatch or turf, with timber or even whalebone supports. The same dry-stone walling techniques have been practised in the north of Scotland ever since, as exemplified by old crofts and farm boundary walls.

Brochs always seem to have been built in easily defensible locations, but they would also have had to be constructed close to the arable land worked by

The remains of some 500 brochs are to be found in northern and western Scotland. This illustration shows a reconstruction of a broch based on surviving examples, such as the impressive Broch of Gurness in Orkney. This broch has two thick walls separated by a small passageway. This space serves as a stairwell that winds its way up to the top of the structure, which provides access to the interior floor levels. The broch has a small entrance, protected by guard chambers, while the lower floor of the structure houses a well and storage pits. The broch is approached through a small village, itself protected by a stone wall, as well as a bivallate arrangement of banks and revetted ditches.

the community who built the structure. In many cases the structures were built close to the sea: Gurness and Midhowe were both built on the Orkney seashore, separated from each other by the waters of Eynhallow Sound. The Broch of Gurness is particularly impressive, because a small settlement of at least six sets of houses was built beneath the tower itself. Each was entered from a main passageway that led through the village to the broch. Some of these buildings were entered from small courtyards, flanked by storage sheds. The result resembled a stone-built warren. Surrounding the village was a substantial stone wall at least two metres high, which may have been surmounted by a stone walkway and parapet. The whole complex was entered through a double gate, reached by a stone-lined approach that spanned a ditch running around the landwards side of the village. Beyond this a series of two banks and ditches completed what must have appeared a most formidable site. The neighbouring broch of Midhowe was smaller, with a less developed defensive system surrounding the tower and settlement.

Structures such as these suggested that the society who built them was one under threat, either from neighbouring communities or more likely from outsiders. Were they built as a reaction to a wave of armed Celtic settlers from the south, or were they symbols of community power in an otherwise stable society? So far archaeologists have failed to provide a clear answer. Whoever built them and for whatever reason, they remain as potent reminders of the Iron Age communities who felt the need to defend themselves in such a dramatic fashion.

The oval perimeter of the hill-fort of St. Catherine's Hill, just outside Winchester, Hampshire. The enclosure (on the right of the picture) slopes gently towards the chalk hill's summit, which is now crowned by a small copse – the site of a medieval chapel. It was constructed around 400 BC, and was occupied until the period of the Roman invasion of Britain. (Courtesy of Marcus Cowper)

Reconstruction of a broch, AD 100

Tour of a fortified site: Danebury

Although every hill-fort is different, the easiest way to understand what they looked like and how they functioned is to conduct a tour of one particular site as it looked in its heyday. Hill-forts remained in use for long periods, often several centuries, so this will do little to explain the development of the site, although it will offer a snapshot of what it would have looked like at one particular stage of its development, just before it fell into disuse. For the purposes of this exercise the small hill-fort at Danebury in Hampshire offers one of the best vehicles; at just 5.3 hectares it is small enough to act as a model for other larger and more complex sites. It has also been comprehensively excavated, so we know a lot about the site compared with other similar forts.

The first hill-fort at Danebury was built around the mid-6th century BC, and although changes were made to the fortifications over the centuries, the hill-fort remained in use until around 100 BC. At that time its occupation came to an abrupt and possibly bloody end. While it is not part of this exercise to provide a detailed account of the changes the hill-fort underwent during this period, a brief outline will help our understanding of the site. Professor Barry Cunliffe who directed its excavation in the 1970s divided the development of Danebury into four phases, the last of which involved the use of the fort in the Sub-Roman Period. Phase 3 represents how the fort would have looked just before its dramatic end, and this is the one we shall focus on here.

The fort sat on a small chalky hilltop above the River Test, 143m above sea level, a few miles to the east of the modern town of Winchester. As the rolling

By the time of the Roman invasion of Britain in the mid-1st century AD, Roman military engineering was highly developed, and so the fortifications the invaders encountered proved relatively easy to capture. This is a detail from Trajan's Column in Rome, showing assault troops, an onager and crew, skirmishers and siegeworks. (Stratford Archive)

downland surrounding the fort was not particularly high, the fort would have been visible for some distance. On a clear day the hill-fort of Beacon Hill can be seen to the north, while to the west the aspect is of the open countryside of Salisbury Plain. The landscape surrounding it would have been open, although extensive woodland lay to the south. The River Test provided water for cattle grazing, while a spring half a mile from the hilltop provided water for the settlement it enclosed. In fact Cunliffe and his team have shown that during the Iron Age Danebury was surrounded by field systems, which date from between 550 and 100 BC – making them contemporary with the fort. The presence of Neolithic barrows in the same area suggests that Danebury was already an important location for the local population long before the hill-fort was built. A chalk road ran eastwards from the main entrance towards a ford over the River Test (where there was a profusion of field boundaries), while a smaller track

circled the outer ditch from the main gate until it reached the most southerly part of the fort; at this point the track then headed south along the rise which led to Wallop Brook, another heavily cultivated area.

Approaching the fort from the river, the most obvious feature of the fortification would be its rampart, a circular chalk bank that stood about five metres above the level of the hillside. It was roughly triangular in section, and was surmounted by a small wooden palisade. The whole bank was approximately eight metres wide at its base, although it narrowed to accommodate a one-metre-wide walkway set at the rear of the palisade itself. Immediately in front of the rampart lay the 'V-shaped' ditch, four metres deep at its centre, and climbing slightly more acutely on its inner face. The ditch itself had been used to quarry stones and chalk rubble to use in the construction or heightening of the rampart behind it, so it was substantial, measuring approximately 10m across. In front of the ditch ran a berm or counterscarp bank, a rounded feature that, at two metres high, would hide the ditch from any attacker, but would be overlooked by defenders standing on the rampart. The defences were not the same all the way around the circumference of the fort. The ramparts on the southern side of the fort

Without exception Celtic fortifications in Britain proved unable to protect themselves from the Romans, who used siege engines firing stone shot to batter a path through their fragile timber palisades. These red sandstone examples of ballista shot were recovered from the Burnswark hill-fort in the Scottish Borders. (National Museums of Scotland)

The small but impressive Scottish hill-fort at White Caterthun, Angus consists of a strongly fortified, rubble-built enclosure, surrounded by two or three concentric, elliptically shaped ramparts, plus an additional eastern enclosure protected by a single bank. It stands less than a mile away from another small hill-fort, Brown Caterthun. (RCAHMS)

As a hill-fort, Danebury in Hampshire is typical of many similar Iron Age fortifications that lie scattered across southern Britain. However, unlike most others the site was thoroughly excavated over a period of 20 years. As a result we now know more about how the hill-fort of Danebury evolved and what it looked like than most contemporary fortified sites in Britain. The inset **A** shows a plan of the earlier fort on the site, while the main illustration shows the hill-fort at the height of its

development, before its sudden abandonment around 120 BC. Shortly after this date the entrance on the south-western corner of the defences (**B**) was sealed off, leaving only one heavily fortified gateway on the fort's north-east corner (**C**). The three sections of ramparts (**D**) show the way the fort developed over the centuries: the simpler defensive works of the site were improved during the Late Iron Age, while the ramparts themselves were progressively heightened and strengthened over the fort's period of occupation, from around 500 BC onwards.

The hill-fort at Old Winchester Hill, Hampshire is sited at one end of a steep-sided ridge. Its oval-shaped defences consist of a single bank and ditch, with an entrance at both the eastern and western sides. The site was clearly an important one before the Iron Age, as several Bronze Age burial mounds are found within the enclosure. (Courtesy of Marcus Cowper)

were less substantial than on the northern face, while the ditch itself narrowed slightly to around eight metres across.

Visitors would approach the eastern entrance to the fort under the gaze of sentinels on the ramparts, where the guards could easily close the large wooden gates at short notice if required, or drive intruders away with a hail of slingshots. The chalky approach road was nine metres wide – enough for two chariots to emerge from the fort side by side. The gate itself was a complicated affair, with two sections of outworks lying in front of the gateway. Even before a visitor reached the entrance an outlying ditch had to be crossed, a wide but shallow trench that encircled the whole hill-fort. Once past this obstacle the visitor would be faced with a series of small banks – essentially the counterscarp of the main ditch that surrounded the fort. These projected out to flank the path, a little like the claws of an insect. However, the ditch ended at the main gate itself, so these spurs formed what is best described as a semi-circular outer enclosure of the fort (see page 27).

The excavations revealed that the gap between the jaws of the bank was sealed by an outer gateway, the exact nature of which is still unclear. Inside this enclosure two second sections of bank provided a further obstacle before the gatehouse was reached, protecting the flanks of the enclosure.

Where the road crossed the inner rampart the banks turned outwards for 20–30m, creating a funnel through which any visitor would have had to pass. This is where the main gateway stood, a structure that was about six metres wide, its approach covered by the projecting hornworks of the ramparts. It was

The early development of a hill-fort: Danebury, 120 BC

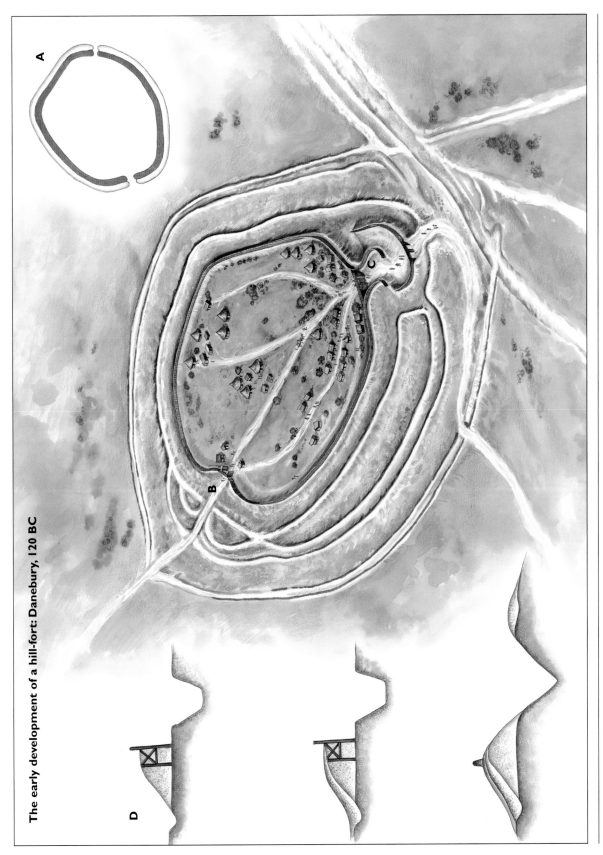

The remains of the stone rampart of White Caterthun hill-fort, Angus. Although it was built within sight of the adjacent Brown Caterthun hill-fort, the latter was built with conventional earthen banks, which suggests a different period of occupation. (Stratford Archive)

Dunsinane Hill, Perthshire – the literary last bastion of Macbeth – is the site of a small Iron Age hill-fort overlooking Strathmore. A thick, stone-filled inner wall was surrounded by two outer ramparts, although many of the fort's features were destroyed by extensive digging by 19th-century antiquarians. (RCAHMS)

a double gate, its two wings opening inwards into the fort itself. There is evidence that some form of tower or gallery structure stood over the gateway, probably linking the two ends of the inner ramparts to form a continuous band of defences. A visitor would have had to pass under this structure to enter the fort itself.

Once through the defences the wide chalky road would lead off into the interior of the fort, narrowing as it went until it reached the far side of the enclosure. Other smaller roads forked off from this main thoroughfare like branches from a tree, two to the left and three to the right. The roads to the left were flanked by rows of square-shaped granaries, probably raised off the ground slightly on nine posts – three on each face and one supporting the centre of the structure. Each side of the building was approximately six metres across, although a few smaller, two metre-wide, four-post granaries or hayrick platforms lay scattered between the larger buildings. Almost certainly each structure contained baskets or ceramic jars filled with wheat, oats or barley. To the right the visitor would have seen the main settlement area of Danebury, with a seemingly irregular scattering of thatched roundhouses that extended as far as the northern side of the earthworks.

The last fork in the road led off towards a shrine or temple structure, built in what was roughly the centre of the whole enclosure. It was a square structure, approximately the same size as the nine-post granary buildings, but of more solid construction, with its walls set into the ground. Three smaller shrines lay a few yards down the path towards the fork in the road, a larger one on the left of the path and two smaller ones to the right. All three were square, the largest being just under three metres across, and the entrances of all three structures faced the visitor as he approached the main temple 10m behind them on the path. Although archaeology cannot definitely say what was held in these shrines, we know from

other evidence that the Celtic people who lived in Danebury would have worshipped a range of deities, and surrounded images of their gods with votive offerings of food, drink or even scraps of cloth. The importance of these structures would have been emphasized by their central position within the Danebury enclosure.

The one thing missing from the picture created by the archaeology of the site is the impression a visitor would have had of the people who lived there. At its height Danebury had a population of between 300 and 500 people, as well as their domestic animals and pets. Chickens would have scratched around the feet of any visitor, while the smell of animals held in wicker enclosures next to the roundhouses would have been pervasive. Sanitation was largely unknown, and human waste was simply deposited in small pits then loosely covered over. From other sources we know what these people would have looked like, and the appearance of the Celts of the Late Iron Age has been covered in other Osprey books (see Men-at-Arms 158, *Rome's Enemies (2): Gallic and British Celts*). However, the general appearance would have been of a fairly wealthy rural economy, and a community that enjoyed both a stable political structure and one which could easily provide for the welfare of its own people. Far from being a primitive settlement, Danebury would have been a well-organized farming community, whose inhabitants enjoyed a reasonably high standard of living, and whose safety was assured by the impressive defensive works that protected their village.

The small moorland hill-fort of Lordenshaws, Northumberland consists of an oval enclosure of about one-third of a hectare surrounded by a substantial double bank and ditch. An ancient trackway still leads to its western entrance (shown here), while the remains of older enclosures and dykes can still be traced outside the fort's perimeter. (Courtesy of Keith Durham)

The living site

Having examined the regional spread of these fortified sites in Iron Age Britain, and looked at the varieties of fortified enclosures built by the Celts or their predecessors, we shall now look at how these fortifications were used by the people who built them, and how well they served as defensive positions in time of danger.

Hill-forts were not mere fortifications. In most cases they also served as a place of habitation for the community who built them. The defensive qualities of the fort might not be tested for decades or even centuries at a time, although the mere presence of the defences would have acted as a deterrent to potentially hostile neighbours. Most hill-forts were in continuous or near continuous use for several centuries, and during this time the shape and nature of the fort would have changed, as too might the size and political status of the community it served. Like any long-lived defensive work, improvements would have been undertaken to reflect changes in warfare and weaponry, such as the introduction of new fort-building techniques or types of missile weapons into Britain. Similarly the interior of the fort would also alter over time, and archaeological excavations on several sites have proved that building types, the organization of the interior and even the size of the settlement were all subject to change.

Maiden Castle

To better understand the way hill-forts developed with the passage of time we could do worse than to look at probably the most famous example: Maiden Castle in Dorset (see pages 38–39). This, the largest hill-fort site in Britain, was subject to two large-scale scientific investigations, allowing us to trace its development and to understand the way it functioned as a settlement with more certainty than many other smaller sites. Maiden Castle was first excavated by Sir Mortimer Wheeler between 1934 and 1937. Further excavations were carried out in 1985–86. It has been proposed that the name probably derived from the pre-Celtic name for the hill-fort, 'Mai Dun', which approximates to 'big fort'. It occupies a prominent saddle-shaped ridge two miles from the town of Dorchester, presenting a striking

The major hill-fort of Traprain Law, East Lothian is still an impressive location, despite the damage caused by 20th-century quarrying. Excavations have shown that the site was occupied after the Roman invasion of southern Scotland in AD 80–81, thereby strengthening the belief that the hill-fort was a stronghold of the Votadani, a tribe who allied themselves with the Romans. (RCAHMS)

The hill-fort of Maiden Castle, Dorset, photographed before Sir Mortimer Wheeler's excavations of the site in the late 1930s. This dramatic site was the largest Iron Age hill-fort ever built in Britain, although traces of earlier occupation have been found stretching back to the fourth millennium BC. (Stratford Archive)

appearance to the visitor. The novelist Thomas Hardy described its appearance with considerable eloquence:

> At one's every step forward it rises higher against the south sky, with an obtrusive personality that compels the senses to regard it and consider … The profile of the whole stupendous ruin, as seen at a distance of a mile eastwards, is clearly cut as that of a marble inlay. It is varied with protruberances, which from hereabouts have the animal aspect of warts, wens, knuckles and hips. It may indeed be likened to an enormous many-limbed organism of an antediluvian time … lying lifeless, and covered with a thin green cloth, which hides its substance, while revealing its contour.[1]

The development of the fortifications

Wheeler's excavation was the first large-scale scientific study of a British hill-fort, and helped shape our understanding of the people who built these fortifications. He proved that the fort was built in several phases, the first being concentrated on the eastern half of the ridge. An earlier Neolithic camp and raised causeway or barrow had already been built on the same site, but by the time the fort-builders arrived around 500 BC the traces of this earlier settlement and bank had all but disappeared. The first fortification consisted of a dog-legged bank and ditch dug across the ridge from roughly north to south, thereby creating an enclosure bounded on its remaining three sides by the steep slope of the ridge's eastern end. The bank was revetted using timber, and pierced by a wooden gateway. Another bank ran around the top of the ridge, and was pierced by a gateway at its eastern end. The enclosure was certainly occupied, as traces of timber enclosures dating from this period have been found there.

During the next century the defences fell into disrepair, the ramparts collapsed and the ditch silted up. However, around 400 BC the locals decided to rebuild their hill-fort, this time extending it to encompass the whole of the ridge, an area of some 18½ hectares (46 acres). The eastern gateway was strengthened with an additional semi-circular ramp and ditch, with the gateway divided into

---

[1] Thomas Hardy, 'A Tryst in an Ancient Earthwork', from *A Changed Man, and Other Tales* (London, 1913).

two channels by a median bank. The ramparts and outlying ditch were extended to the western side of the ridge, where a second entrance was constructed, again with a semi-circular line of outer works. Both ramparts were pierced by two gateways approximately 50m apart. This phase of the development of Maiden Castle has been linked to the cultural phase known in Iron Age archaeology as 'A Culture', namely the first identifiable British culture of the Iron Age. Although these people took advantage of the new iron-making technology imported from the mainland of Europe, it is now thought that the majority of these people were indigenous inhabitants of the region.

Around the same time as Maiden Castle was expanded a new group appeared in southern England, their route traced by the remains of their distinctive pottery, the use of the sling and their own particular ideas about fortification. These people were clearly identifiable as Celts.

Around 250 BC these members of 'B Culture', as they are known, began to make their mark on Maiden Castle; its defences went through an extensive revision. As an offensive weapon the sling proved superior in both range and firepower to the javelin used by the 'A Culture' inhabitants. Whether this defensive improvement was made by the old group or the new is largely unknown, but the new scheme was certainly designed to counter and to take advantage of the sling's capabilities. On the northern side of the ridge a secondary bank and ditch was created, supported by a smaller spur bank on the north-western face of the ridge to screen the western gateway. On the south side of the ridge two banks and ditches were added, in addition to additional bank defences in front of both gateways, designed to funnel attackers into a 'killing zone' for slingshot. Finally the original inner rampart was repaired and heightened, the extra scale of the bank supported by a stone revetment buried on the inner face of the earthen bank.

The final form of Maiden Castle's formidable array of defences was probably completed at some stage during the early 1st century BC. The ramparts were enlarged once again, while a substantial counterscarp bank was added which encircled the whole ridge. What was most significant about this third phase of improvements was the strengthening of the two gateways. On the eastern end the outlying defences of the old gateway were filled in or demolished, and in their place a series of two large fortified ramparts were added, both fronted by a ditch and a smaller counterscarp bank. On the western end of Maiden

Castle the old defences were greatly strengthened, and augmented by another outlying rampart, ditch and counterscarp ditch. In addition smaller banks within the gateway complex acted as barriers to funnel attackers trying to round the last outlying rampart before the gatehouse.

The twin gateways themselves were greatly strengthened with stone revetments, as was the north-western entrance to the gateway where it passed the first line of the outer defences. Between the twin gates and the first outer rampart a row of guard huts housed the gate garrison, suggesting a level of military organization that had been lacking in previous defensive systems. In most of the outer ditches leading to the gatehouse (and possibly elsewhere around the fort perimeter) wooden stakes were emplaced as *chevaux de frise*, obstacles designed to deter or hinder any attacker. Finally, firing platforms may well have been installed at various points along the outer ramparts, leading to the gatehouse, so that a 'forlorn hope' of slingers could shoot into the flanks or rear of an assault party. By now Maiden Castle had developed into what was probably the best-defended hill-fort in Britain.

Around the time these final improvements were being made to the defences a new group arrived in southern England. Known as 'C Culture' people, these incomers were Celts of the tribe known as the Belgae, whose origins lay in what is now northern France and southern Belgium. Within half a century these incomers had extended their control over most of south-east England, and by AD 25 at the latest this had extended as far as Maiden Castle, which they may well have occupied. Certainly their influence was felt within the fort. The Belgae, or those who adopted their ways, repaired the ramparts by reinforcing the banks with a layer of earth and strengthened the wall walk and palisade that surmounted it. Strangely enough this palisade was mounted on the inner side of the rampart, leaving the men who patrolled it exposed to fire from outside the fort. This has been explained as being more of a security barrier than a defensive work – controlling access to the ramparts as a privilege reserved for the warrior elite of the garrison. The posts supporting this palisade were sunk deep into the outer edge of the bank, and so in effect they doubled as a reinforcement for the stone revetment buried in the bank itself.

The main eastern gateway of Maiden Castle, Dorset is one of the most complex of any Iron Age hill-fort, with no fewer than four lines of defence outlying the inner rampart and gate, providing three opportunities to pour fire into an attacker's flank before he reached the gate itself. (RCAHM)

These improvements did not help the defenders when they encountered Vespasian's II Legion in AD 43. Maiden Castle was captured without much difficulty by the legionary commander, who would soon become a Roman emperor. After capturing the hill-fort the Romans destroyed the fort's gateways, leaving it defenceless. The site remained occupied for another three decades, until the Romans established a new regional capital two miles away in Durnovaria (Dorchester), named after the local tribe known as the Durotrigii. Around AD 70 Maiden Castle was abandoned, and its once formidable defences became a place of pasture. The Romans had one final humiliation for this great symbol of Celtic power. In AD 313 Christianity became the official religion of the Roman Empire, and around AD 380 a small square temple was built on the eastern side of the ridge, within the bounds of the original fort. A large circular shrine was then built beside what was once the main thoroughfare of the hill-fort, occupying a site that may once have belonged to the principal Celtic roundhouse in the fort. Both structures had fallen into disuse by the end of the 5th century AD.

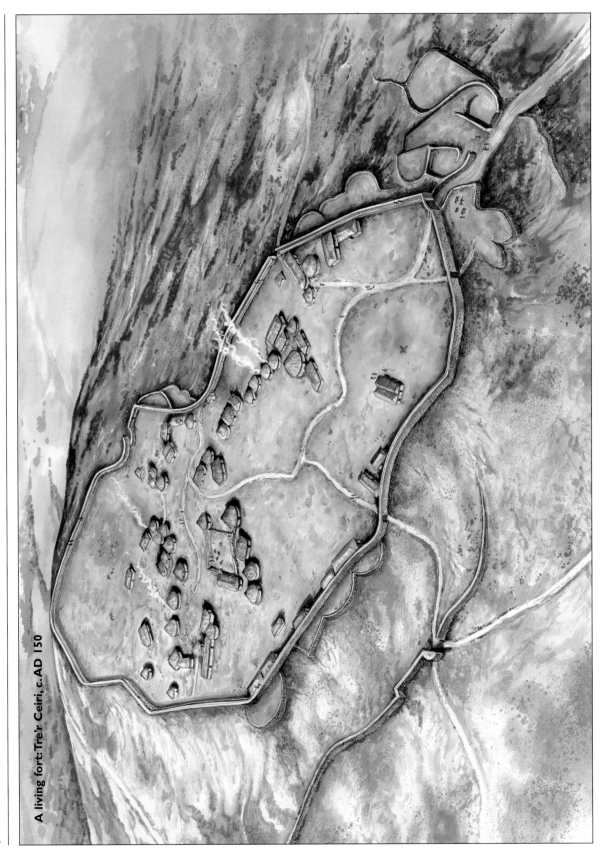

A living fort: Tre'r Ceiri, c. AD 150

A living fort: Tre'r Ceiri, c. AD 150

This unique, stone-built hill-fort crowns the summit of the easternmost of the three peaks of Yr Eifl, on the Llyn Peninsula. The area enclosed by the fort's stone walls is about four hectares, and the walls themselves are in good condition. The archaeological evidence suggests that the fort was built around 100 BC, at the end of the Late Iron Age, and remained in use until the end of the period of Roman occupation of Britain. The remains of some 150 Celtic roundhouses have been found on the site, which suggests it was once the centre of an isolated but thriving community, perched on the very edge of Roman-occupied Britain. The defences of the fort were not greatly strengthened over time, but rather a series of small outworks were added – guardhouses that covered the steep approach roads to the top of the summit. The remains of wall-ringed field enclosures surround the fort, proving that Tre'r Ceiri remained the centre of a thriving agrarian community throughout its period of occupation, and that its population increased significantly during the 1st century AD, probably through the arrival of refugees fleeing the Romans.

The settlement

The one feature that both excavations at Maiden Castle failed to reveal in any detail was the configuration of the hill-fort's interior. After all, the reason the fortifications existed in the first place was to protect the Iron Age community who lived and worked there. Archaeology has revealed a little about how these people lived, and how their settlement was organized. The first settlement there was a Neolithic one, established around 4000 BC. However, the community there was relatively small – probably no more than 100 people, based on the size of the causeway camp they built. It seems to have remained a focus for the Neolithic people of South Dorset, as about 3500 BC the long bank barrow was built, suggesting the ridge was seen as a centre of religious importance. The area was abandoned a few centuries later, and it was not until the very end of the Neolithic period, around 2250 BC, that archaeologists have been able to trace any further activity. During the Bronze Age there seems to have been little occupation, although the nearby Frome Valley became a relatively well-populated area. This all changed around 500 BC, when the Iron Age people of the region built their hill-fort there.

Although little trace remains of the settlements created by either the Neolithic settlers or their early Iron Age ancestors, by comparing Maiden Castle with other sites in the area we can see that there seemed to be a tendency for communities to congregate into easily defended settlements during this period, probably due to an increased level of social unrest. The trouble with Maiden Castle is that the

Traces of damaged features can be found amid the heather covering the entrance to the hill-fort at Lordenshaws, Northumberland. These suggest that the twin banks were once revetted by stone, although the ramparts were subsequently damaged by later settlement during the Dark Ages. (Courtesy of Keith Durham)

An unusual feature of the small circular hill-fort at Lordenshaws is that the site is encircled by several small curving banks, while the sides of the track way leading to the fort itself were once partially revetted with stones. It has been suggested that these outer works were used to house livestock, while the inner enclosure was used as a fortified farm. (Courtesy of Keith Durham).

ridge itself was farmed during the centuries preceding its excavation, while the hill was also used as a source of stone for local building work. This agriculture and quarrying disturbed much of the fragile evidence left behind by these early people, and only the barest clues remain to suggest how their settlement might have looked. Fortunately we can draw parallels between Maiden Castle and other nearby forts. For example during the late Bronze Age evidence of trade and manufacture can be found in many communities in that part of England. By the time the Iron Age people built their hill-fort much of this activity had ceased, and the people reverted to a purely agrarian economy. Consequently grain storage became important, and the ability to store produce in locations such as hill-forts suggests an increasing level of centralized control over the population. In other words Maiden Castle probably acted as a seat of government for a local tribe, whose influence extended down the Frome Valley to the south-east, and southwards towards the coast at Portland.

There is evidence that the land within this hinterland was extensively farmed during the Iron Age, and that it was considered of good quality. The development of so many hill-forts in the Dorset area during the early Iron Age suggests that this land was contested by neighbouring communities. It was therefore a time of upheaval, when the inhabitants of Maiden Castle needed the security offered by a well-defended hill-fort settlement rather than by scattered farmsteads and unprotected villages.

The earliest traces of structures within the enclosure of Maiden Castle date from around 400 BC, when the hill-fort was expanded to encompass the entire ridge. A series of limited excavations have gone some way to showing how the site developed, but in many cases, where geophysics rather than excavation has to be relied upon, it is impossible to say what structures date from this mid-Iron Age phase of occupation and which were built later. It does appear that the large and slightly ridged plateau that made up the enclosure contained a central metalled road running close to but not along the spine of the ridge, with what might have been non-metalled side roads radiating outwards from the eastern gateway. It seemed the inhabitants avoided building either roadways or structures on the line of the Neolithic barrow, probably out of respect for the dead they imagined lay beneath it.

Archaeologists believe that during the initial stages of the fort's occupation settlement was concentrated near the median ridge of the fort, leaving a lot of open space towards the edges of the ridge. The settlement then expanded outwards. The only clear evidence of these earlier phases has been the discovery of a number of rubbish pits and post-holes in the centre of the fort. Traces of a 'four-poster' hut was discovered – a rectangular structure which has also been found in other Late Iron Age sites, particularly in the hill-forts around the Welsh border. It has been suggested that these structures were too small to represent houses, so it is surmised that the buildings were storage barns. However, it has also been suggested that because these structures were concentrated near the ramparts of the fort they could be watchtowers of some sort, or even platforms built to honour the dead.

We are on firmer ground in the later phases of occupation. Geophysical surveys have shown that an irregular scattering of timber and thatch roundhouses occupied the bulk of the site, interspersed with storage pits and refuse dumps. The

Dunsapie Crag in Holyrood Park in Edinburgh is a small volcanic plug that was surmounted by a tiny Iron Age hill-fort, enclosed within a single bank. Traces of two roundhouses can be seen inside the enclosure, while evidence of contemporary field systems have been found close to the site. (RCAHMS)

excavation conducted during the 1980s also revealed a little more about the occupation of the fort, and a number of these roundhouses were excavated.

The remains of three huts were discovered in 1986, the largest of which measured almost six metres in diameter. These structures were typical of the huts associated with the Iron Age in Britain: wooden circular structures, surrounded by a slight ditch and bank. The building was centred on an open hearth, while traces of an oven were found to one side of this. The main structural timbers of the dwelling consisted of a circle of upright posts holding up a frame of timber beams. The entrance to the hut faced south, and was delineated by a small fence leading onto a limestone walkway. A post-hole suggests that the entrance was once secured by a substantial wooden door. The excavating team also discovered that the structure was in use for a long time, and was rebuilt at least three times during its occupancy.

Cultivation and quarrying has destroyed much of the evidence of other huts on top of the plateau, so all we can do is imagine that during the Late Iron Age the hill-fort contained numerous structures of this type. After all, experimental archaeologists and re-enactors have proved that a hut of the size mentioned above could comfortably house an extended family group of around six adults and children. Given the correlation between the size of the hill-fort and the population it housed discussed previously, we arrive at a projected total of just over 180 huts, housing over a thousand people. This number of buildings seems high, given the need to provide additional space for storage facilities and refuse pits, not to mention workshops, communal buildings and religious centres within the same enclosure.

In the decades before the Roman invasion these underground storage and refuse pits were filled in, an action which may well reflect the influence of the 'C Culture' people within the fort. They were replaced with storage barns, which improved the capacity and the suitability of grain storage within the hill-fort. Even more spectacularly, the huts appear to have been reorganized. Rather than being scattered around the ridge, they were concentrated into rows, a little like modern suburban streets, with each roundhouse enclosure spaced evenly, and far closer to each other than before. A row of three such houses has been uncovered, including one built using stone. The middle house of the three was built on the foundations of an earlier structure, and was even terraced slightly to take advantage of the natural slope. The final house of the three was surrounded by a small gully. All three structures appear to have been repaired during their occupancy, which suggests they remained in use for some considerable time – probably surviving beyond the period of Roman invasion in the mid-1st century AD, roughly a century after the structures were first built.

Maiden Castle, England, AD 43

Maiden Castle is the largest and best-known hill-fort in Britain, its multivallate defences dominating the Dorset countryside. The site is shown as it would have looked at the time of the Roman invasion of Britain in AD 43, when it was almost certainly attacked by a Roman legion. By that stage its defences consisted of a formidable series of banks and ditches, the last of which – the inner rampart of the fort – ran around the edge of the ridge on which the fort stood. A series of archaeological investigations of the site in the 1930s and the 1980s has revealed a lot about how the fort would have looked in this period, when it provided a safe haven for a community of as many as 1,000 people. Granaries and storage chambers occupy the outer parts of the enclosure, while the main habitation area is concentrated towards the centre of the site. The hill-fort is dominated by the complex defences of its two gateways, the most impressive of which is the formidable eastern gateway in the lower right (an earlier version of which is shown in the upper right inset). The series of outer banks and ditches was designed to break up any attack, and to expose the attackers to a hail of javelins and slingshots from both firing platforms on the outer works, and the fighting platform that ringed the inner rampart. It has been suggested that the roundhouses in front of the gateway served as guard huts.

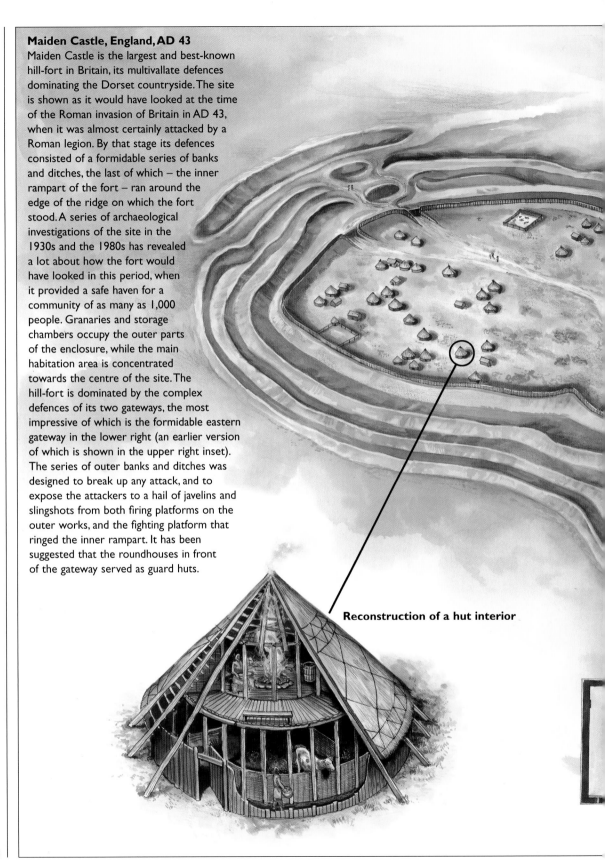

Reconstruction of a hut interior

An earlier form of the eastern gateway

Roundhouses

Timber 'sentry' platforms

Temple

House

Floor plan of the later Roman temple
and house located in this area (c. AD 380)

This reorganization of the houses suggests a major social change at Maiden Castle. Firstly, it shows that whoever was in charge of the community was able to change the basic structure of everyday life for what he or she probably saw as the greater good. Archaeologist and the 1986 excavation director Niall Sharples argued that:

> The construction of regimented rows of houses may have been an attempt to break down the extended kinship ties of individual families and strengthen the importance of the larger urban community. The variation of house design, however, suggests that the identity of the individuals had not been totally absorbed by whatever collective ideals were in force and is in marked contrast to the situation in some other hill-forts.

This reorganization of the enclosure inevitably involved a major upheaval for the community, and for the first time the presence of residential and communal areas can be traced within the interior of the hill-fort. Large areas appear to have been devoted to grain storage, as the remains of storage barns – the structures which replaced the earlier grain storage pits – have been discovered. It seems as if the people who ran the community wanted to be able to feed a larger population than normal in the event of an attack, or needed additional grain to feed a workforce brought in from the surrounding countryside to help improve the defences of the hill-fort. Grain storage also helped provide a means of currency and exchange in the rural Iron Age economy, and its presence would have helped encourage the creation of specialized trades and industries, where labour was paid in either cash or grain. After all, the Belgae used coinage, which suggests that by the time the Romans arrived the economy of Maiden Castle was based both on agrarian production and on trade and manufacture, thereby mirroring the activity found in the region during the Bronze Age.

After the Roman invasion of AD 43 and the slighting of the gatehouse defences by the Roman army, this well-organized social structure appears

The Iron Age Broch of Midhowe is located on the shore of the Orkney island of Rousay. Like the nearby broch settlement at Gurness, it is surrounded by stone outbuildings, protected by an outlying stone-revetted bank. (Historic Scotland)

to have broken down. For the next few decades the population appeared to decline steadily, and buildings were once again scattered across the site rather than grouped together in streets. Only one house from this period was firmly identified in the 1980s, but it is clear that some if not most of the later 'suburban' houses fell into disuse. Other evidence of occupation is sparse, although Professor Wheeler uncovered the remains of five houses and several storage pits as well as an iron-working area that he associated with the period immediately after the Roman invasion. There was also evidence that the settlement spilled out through the disused eastern gateway and that buildings were established within the banks of the fort's outworks beyond the gate. At the same time many of the outlying ditches were filled, suggesting a change of emphasis from defence to accessibility. The settlement was abandoned a few decades later, as the regional centre of power shifted two miles east to the new Roman *civitas peregrina* (regional capital) of Durnovaria (Dorchester).

The economic and political centre

Maiden Castle served an agrarian community, and so farming rather than trade or manufacture was of primary importance to the people who lived there. However, it also served as an important urban centre that dominated the surrounding region, and traces of its political and economic power have been discovered. Food production increased during the Iron Age as new farm tools and techniques helped improve crop yield, particularly of wheat and barley. At the same time archaeologists have shown that livestock was farmed within the area of Maiden Castle, and the remains of cattle, sheep, pigs and chickens have all been found within the hill-fort enclosure, along with the remains of dogs, goats and wild animals (deer and hare). This all suggests that food was readily available at Maiden Castle during the Iron Age, and that neighbouring farmers would probably drive their livestock or transport their grain to the site where it would be exchanged, sold or handed over as a form of taxation.

Maiden Castle was well placed as a manufacturing centre, as local supplies of copper and tin ore were available within its hinterland. Archaeologists have recovered substantial quantities of bronze and iron tools, and although there is no evidence that bronze objects were ever produced within the hill-fort, Professor Wheeler did detect signs that bronze was being reworked at a workshop located in the south-west corner of the fort. Iron was certainly manufactured on the site, but the only clear evidence for this is in the period after the Roman invasion. It is more likely that iron tools and other objects were manufactured in specialist centres elsewhere, and then brought to Maiden Castle as objects for barter. There is evidence that pottery was produced within the confines of the fort, as the remains of clay-baking ovens were discovered. However, Maiden Castle lacked a ready supply of water, and so other better-placed locations were probably used to supply its inhabitants, who purchased the ceramic goods they needed in exchange for agricultural produce. The only industry that may well have thrived on the site was textile production, a business which left little in the way of surviving evidence apart from bone tools used in the treatment of wool, as well as bobbins, pins and needles.

Without industry or a religious centre it can be argued that Maiden Castle was not much of a settlement. It imported most of its manufactured goods from elsewhere, and what it did produce was probably just enough to supply its own population. Archaeologists have described settlements such as these as proto-urban – population centres that rely almost exclusively on an agrarian economy for their survival. This means Maiden Castle might have been a substantial settlement wielding considerable influence over its hinterland, but it was not a town in the accepted sense. It is better viewed as a fortified rural community, which explains why it was so easily overshadowed by the establishment of a permanent Roman township offering all the trading opportunities that Maiden Castle lacked.

Celtic fortifications in operation

Hill-forts today are deceptive places: the smooth, grass-covered banks and ditches have been rounded and weathered over the centuries, and the approach to them, although often something of a climb, is no longer an experience fraught with danger. It would have been a different story at the height of the Late Iron Age, where the ramparts would have been steeper and higher, the ditches impassable, and the ramparts lined with well-armed defenders. Stakes and impedimenta would hinder any approach over the outer banks and ditches of the fort, while the main gate itself would present a labyrinthine trap to an unwary enemy.

The principles of defence

The most basic form of defensive work was a simple timber palisade, often associated with a bank and outlying ditch. Archaeological evidence shows that these were usually built by sinking a series of upright posts into the top of the bank, then linking these together to form a rail-type fence. This then supported the upright stakes that formed the frontage of the palisade. In almost all known examples the timbers were slotted, pegged or tied together; the use of iron nails was extremely rare. Naturally enough the only surviving evidence of these structures is the post-holes, although in a few cases traces of the palisade itself have been detected. Many Iron Age or Late Bronze Age fortifications appear to have begun as a palisaded enclosure, and were only developed into more complex defended sites later. For example, at Dinorben in Conwy a line of 5th-century BC post-holes was found beneath the rampart, suggesting a palisade predated the existing bank. Some of these palisades have been dated as early as the 8th century BC, some three centuries before the appearance of the conventional rampart and ditch hill-forts.

A development of the basic palisade was the box rampart, where a double line of posts was sunk into a bank, some two or three metres apart, then 'laced' together to form a wooden frame. The structure was then filled with soil to create a solid rampart. The defences of Hod Hill, Dorset were built using this method. At Danebury, Hampshire, archaeologists discovered that the fort was

Like Midhowe, the Broch of Gurness is another Iron Age settlement built on the Orkney seashore, although the whole enclosed area is considerably larger and more complex. It was surrounded by stone wall, and then by an outlying double bank and ditch. (Historic Scotland)

originally built using this box method, but at a later date the original structure was replaced by a large earthen bank.

Building a rampart without a box structure appears to have developed during the Early Iron Age, although a simple timber revetment was sometimes used to hold the earth or stone in place when the bank was being built. An example of this type of construction is found at Cissbury, Sussex, a large 20-hectare site where the palisade formed the outer retaining wall of an earthen bank behind it. These earthen banks tended to be higher than earlier structures, with a steeper outer face to make it harder for an attacker to reach the palisade or breastwork at the top of the rampart. Similarly a steep inner face to the rampart was easier to construct, as it reduced the amount of soil that had to be moved. At Wandlebury, Cambridgeshire, the earlier box structure was converted into an outer defensive line, while a larger timber-fronted bank was built that resembled the one found at Cissbury. What these remains fail to provide is any solid evidence for the palisade or breastwork that ran along the top of the rampart. Presumably the timber revetment doubled as a palisade, as it was higher than the bank formed behind it.

Although stone-built ramparts were very different in appearance to earthen ones, a similar approach was adopted. The hill-fort at Tre'r Ceiri in Caernarfon was surrounded by a stone-built rampart where the outer face also formed the palisade. A stone walkway ran behind this outer face, and the wall then descended towards the interior of the enclosure by means of two stepped revetments or terraces, which imparted greater strength to the whole structure. A more complex stone rampart is found at Worlebury in Somerset, where archaeologists have shown that the original complex of walls once stood to a height of over 10m. As at Tre'r Ceiri the main rampart was supported by a series of stone revetments or terraces stepping down towards the interior of the fort, while the outer face presented a near vertical face to any attacker. In effect this strengthened the defence, because even if the outer wall were damaged, the stone revetments behind would serve as secondary walls, thus maintaining the integrity of the defence.

A variation of the conventional stone rampart is found in the 'vitrified' forts of Scotland, where the walls were deliberately subjected to the effects of fire. The process of setting fire to the structure fused the rocks together in various degrees, and in some cases produced a distinctive glass-like coating that served as a binding agent. Examples include the Tap O'Noth on Bennachie, Grampian; Barry Hill, Perthshire; and Craig Phadrig outside Inverness. Similar vitrified structures were found in Ireland and in Central Europe, but outside Scotland they are not found elsewhere on the British mainland. In many cases the vitrified walls were then reinforced or revetted by unvitrified stone, often built up on both the outer and inner faces of the vitrified rampart.

However strong the ramparts of an Iron Age fort were, the weakest point of the site was always the gateway – and it was presumably there that an attacker would concentrate his efforts. Obviously the builders placed great emphasis on strengthening the gateway defences, usually by placing obstacles in front of them, which would channel an attack into killing zones where the defenders could shower the

The interior of the Broch of Gurness is divided into small compartments, built around a central hearth (in the lower right of the illustration). The presence of a well and storage pits suggests the broch was built primarily for defence, an impression heightened by the low doorway, protected by small guard chambers. (Historic Scotland)

attackers with javelins and slingshot stones. The simplest form of gateway would be an open entrance, sealed with a temporary barrier such as cut logs or felled trees. Usually the passage through the rampart was faced with stone, then blocked by one or more wooden gates. Maiden Castle appears to have had two gateways, separated by a short length of rampart. In some forts, such as Dinorben, a gatehouse or guard post lay behind the gate itself, which suggests the presence of a permanent gate garrison. At Maiden Castle one of two small guard posts located at the eastern entrance was equipped with a hearth, which supports the theory that these posts were permanently manned.

One surprising aspect is the lack of iron fittings associated with Iron Age gateways. At South Cadbury, Somerset, and Hembury, Devon, iron rings were found which might well have formed part of a gate hinge. It appears that in most cases these hinges, like the gates and gateposts themselves, were constructed using wood. The width of the gateway seems to have varied considerably; at Danebury in Hampshire the gate itself had two leaves or sides, and was supported in the centre by a post set into a stone-lined post-hole. At Bredon Hill, Gloucestershire the gateway spanned a 5m-wide road, and was constructed in a similar fashion to Danebury. What is interesting about both these gateways is that both were set between long passageways, formed by the ramparts turning outward (at Danebury) or inward (at Bredon Hill). Defenders on the ramparts could therefore shower the approach to the gate with stones even more effectively than they could when defending a more conventional gateway system. At Bredon Hill it appears that the line of ramparts was spanned by a footbridge which crossed the approach road, while the gateway itself was set some 20m further back, at the end of the inward-turning horns of the bank. Some archaeologists have suggested that these gateways or footbridges were decorated with trophies of war such as severed heads or skulls, or augmented by some form of triumphal arch. However, the evidence for these features is either circumstantial or non-existent.

The gateway itself was usually approached through a series of outer works, which were designed to make the attackers turn and expose their side to the defenders. If the attacker was equipped with a shield then a left-hand turn in the

The Broch of Mousa in Shetland is the most impressive broch structure to survive, its walls still standing to a height of 13m. The small doorway on the left of the structure was its only entrance. (Stratford Archive)

approach meant they would lose the protection of the shield as they advanced. At Hod Hill the approach involved a turn to the right, which suggests that an unfinished outwork in front of the main gate was probably intended to provide a forwards fighting position for the defenders, where they could assault the attackers in the rear and right flank as they advanced towards the gate. At St Catherine's Hill in Hampshire the approach to the gateway was free from any such obstructions, but post-holes on either side of the entrance suggest a walkway might have projected forward to flank the gate itself in a fashion similar to the hornworks found at Danebury.

An additional obstacle was sometimes used in the form of *chevaux de frise*; these were wooden stakes embedded in ditches or banks to slow the advance of any attacker, who would have to thread through the stakes. In Wales and Scotland jagged rocks were used as an alternative to wooden stakes, while in a few sites in Wales such as Pen-y-Gaer in Conwy boulders were strewn outside the perimeter to achieve the same effect. In short the people of Iron Age Britain used every means they could to place an attacker at a disadvantage: building their forts on hilltops, creating networks of banks and ditches, constructing complex entrances, and placing additional obstacles in the path of any attack. As such they used all the principles of defence that could be found in later periods. Their only limitation lay in the manner in which these Celtic peoples fought, and in the limited weaponry available to them. As long as they faced opponents from a similar culture, their fortifications were virtually impregnable. However, when they encountered a technologically superior opponent the weaknesses of these defensive systems were exposed, and they proved as defensible as a medieval castle attacked by Renaissance artillery, or stone-built Victorian forts bombarded by modern rifled ordnance.

The defence of a hill-fort

The Celtic fortifications of Britain were certainly not designed to withstand an attack by a professional standing army such as the one fielded by Rome in the 1st century AD. The Greek historian Strabo said of the Celts that they 'were war mad, high spirited, and quick to battle, but otherwise straightforward, and not of evil character'. By necessity the way they designed their fortifications was influenced by the manner in which they waged war. In particular, their ability to defend brochs, hill-forts or other fortified sites depended on their tactical ability, their available weapons, and their skill in using them.

It is important to consider the weapons at their disposal in order to understand what part these played in the defence of a fortified position. We know from the writings of Roman historians such as Caesar, Tacitus, Dio and Suetonius among others how the Celts fought, and what weapons they used. The principal missile weapon in use in Britain was the sling, which fired a small round stone a distance of up to 60m. Although primarily a hunting weapon, it could also be used in time of war. The large caches of slingshot stones recovered from several hill-forts are clear indications that these weapons were considered crucial in the defence of a fortified position. An opponent would rarely be killed by a slingshot, but the stone it fired could break bones or crack skulls. A harassing fire could be aimed at an approaching force, and as the attackers clambered over the outer lines of banks and ditches they would be slowed, thus remaining in optimum range for longer than if their approach went unhampered.

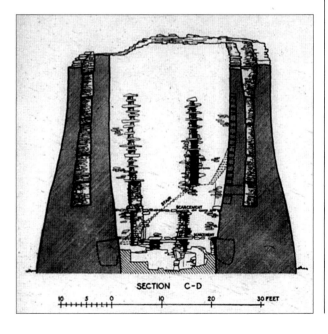

A section of the Broch of Mousa shows how the walls were double-skinned above ground level, allowing space for the stairway between the two walls. As at Gurness, the ground floor contained wells and storage pits. (Stratford Archive)

SECTION C-D

Hill-fort gates: Dinorben, c.500–100 BC

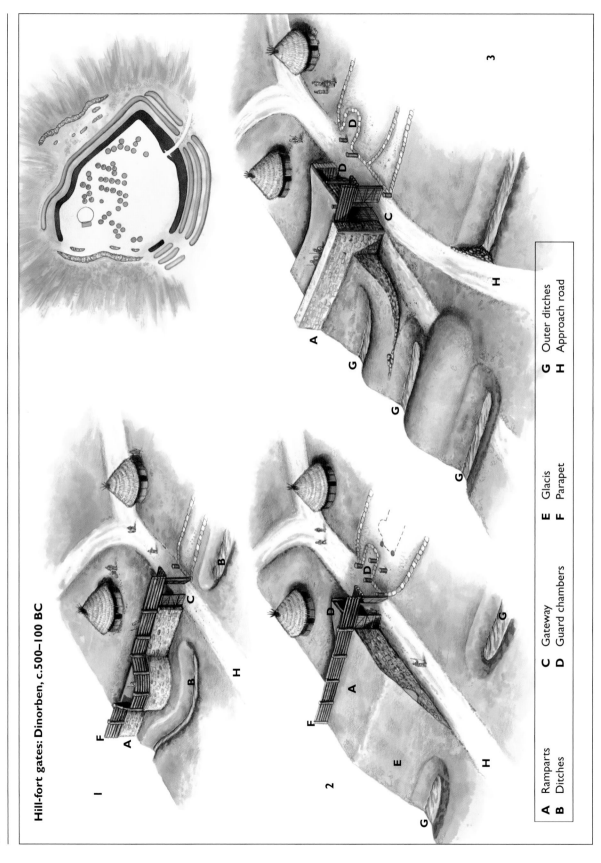

A Ramparts
B Ditches
C Gateway
D Guard chambers
E Glacis
F Parapet
G Outer ditches
H Approach road

Hill-fort gates: Dinorben, c.500–100 BC

The hill-fort of Dinorben, Wales made the best possible use of the natural defences of the site on which it was built, protected on three sides by a steep escarpment, as shown in the plan view at top right. The remaining side was protected by a thick stone rampart and three outlying ditches. The site was excavated on three occasions, and this information allows us to reconstruct the three phases of development of the fort's gateway. In the first phase (**1**) a simple stone-fronted wall was built around a timber-laced frame, although there is evidence that this structure replaced an earlier wooden palisade, bank and ditch. A bulwark on one side of the gate provided a convenient platform for the defenders. During the next phase (**2**) the original walls were extensively widened to around 10m, protected by a stone-filled earthen glacis. The gateway itself was flanked by two guard chambers, while a deep ditch encircled the landward side of the fort. In the final phase (**3**) the stone ramparts of the fort were heightened to create a breastwork, while additional ditches were cut in front of the gateway. The approach to the gateway was revetted using stone, and angled so that any attacker would have to expose his unshielded side to the defenders' fire as he approached.

Once the enemy reached the last ditch they would be within javelin range. Although they were slow in flight, if enough light throwing spears were thrown at a target the barrage would almost certainly cause casualties, being difficult to avoid. Given that they were usually thrown overarm from a rampart against troops approaching the firer from below, they were difficult weapons to aim with any effect. Instead they should be considered more of an indirect fire weapon – a last form of defensive fire before the attackers reached the rampart or gateway. Finally, the defenders would throw whatever they had to hand, such as piles of rocks. Once the attackers had scaled the bank and had reached the rampart, the fighting would be hand-to-hand, using spear, sword and shield. Bows were almost certainly used as hunting weapons by the Celts in Britain, although they appear to have been fairly rare. Strangely there is no account of them being used as a military weapon.

The practical limitations of these weapons influenced the way the Celts built fortifications. After all, the people who built the brochs and hill-forts of Celtic Britain almost certainly had no experience of the Roman way of war, and had no inkling of the vast technological gap between their defensive methods and the Roman form of siege warfare, with its secure fortified camps, siege engines and concentrated bombardments. They built to defend themselves against what they knew – raids by fellow Celts, or even large-scale assaults a determined tribal enemy. This meant maintaining a well-defended perimeter, and encircling this with man-made or natural terrain designed to hinder an attacker, either by forcing them to endure a rain of missiles as they approached the inner ramparts, or by tiring them as they struggled to climb up towards the waiting defenders. Given these parameters, hill-forts appear to have been successful in doing what they were designed for. Although we know less about how brochs were defended, their similarity to later Norman keeps or even Border Reiver strongholds speaks volumes about the practicality of their design.

We know a little about the type of warfare for which the great hill-forts were built from Julius Caesar, who described Celtic siege tactics as they existed in the mid-1st century BC. His comments are brief but revealing:

> There was a town of the Remi, by name Bibrax, eight miles distant from this camp. This the Belgae on their march began to attack with great vigour. [The assault] was with difficulty sustained for that day. The Gauls' mode of besieging is the same as that of the Belgae: when after having drawn a large number of men around the whole of the fortifications, stones

Archaeological evidence suggests that the interior of the Broch of Mousa was once divided by wooden floors. Access to each level was through a narrow stone stairway built between the outer and inner skins of the wall. The stair ended in a wall walk, although it appears the whole structure was once covered by a conical timber and thatched roof. (Historic Scotland)

have begun to be cast against the wall on all sides, and the wall has been stripped of its defenders, [then], forming a *testudo*, they advance to the gates and undermine the wall: which was easily effected on this occasion; for while so large a number were casting stones and darts, no one was able to maintain his position upon the wall. When night had put an end to the assault, Iccius, who was then in command of the town, one of the Remi, a man of the highest rank and influence among his people, and one of those who had come to Caesar as ambassador [to sue] for peace, sends messengers to him, [to report] 'That, unless assistance were sent to him he could not hold out any longer.' (*The Gallic Wars*)

Caesar duly marched to the aid of the Remi and destroyed the Belgae in battle. The account might well have been written a century before the hill-forts of Britain faced an attack by the Romans, but the tribal warfare for which the forts were designed would hardly have changed much. The mention that the attackers assaulted the gate is particularly revealing, as the evidence from Danebury and several other forts suggests that the gateway was the weak point of the defences. Once the defenders could reach it they would be able to set it on fire, which might well have been what happened at Danebury. Of course Caesar's comment that the Celts formed a *testudo* (or 'tortoise', an attacking formation used by the Roman army) is misleading. It was simply the best means he had of describing a dense assault column of Celtic warriors.

A problem with descriptions of the Celtic forts of Britain and the way they were attacked or defended is that we must rely on a mixture of non-Celtic observers, and often fragmentary or misleading archaeological evidence. The combination of the two can sometimes have dramatically misleading results. During his excavations of Maiden Castle Sir Mortimer Wheeler became convinced that the hill-fort had been attacked by the Romans, who stormed their way into the fort's eastern gateway. He had good reason to be convinced, as the hill-fort stood directly in the path of the Roman invasion, and his team uncovered the remains of what he thought were war graves.

In AD 43 the Roman II (Augusta) Legion advanced rapidly through southern England, led by its commander, the future Roman emperor Vespasian. According to his biographer, Vespasian subdued 'two very formidable tribes and over 20 towns' (or rather hill-forts), one of which was probably Maiden Castle; the tribes were probably the Belgae and the Durotrigii. By the time the Romans reached Maiden Castle the defenders had prepared themselves as best they could;

Dun Carloway (Dun Charlabhaigh) is another small but well-preserved Late Iron Age broch, whose remains perch spectacularly above Loch Roag on Lewis. The broch was damaged during a 16th-century Highland feud when it was used as a hideout, but the double-skinned nature of its wall construction is all the more clearly shown by the ruinous condition. (Historic Scotland)

archaeologists have found the remains of substantial caches of stone shot for slings, the majority of which appear to have been gathered from nearby Chesil Beach. Sir Mortimer Wheeler argued that Vespasian would have crossed the River Frome where Dorchester now stands, and having seen how formidable the western defences were, ordered his legion to concentrate in front of the eastern gate. The hill-fort, described by the historian Leonard Cottrell in 1958 as the work of a 'Vauban of the Iron Age', would indeed have looked formidable. In his report on the excavations published in 1943, Wheeler described what he thought occurred next:

> First the regiment of artillery which usually accompanied a legion was ordered into action and put down a barrage of ballista arrows. The arrows have been found about the site, and buried amongst the outworks, as was a man with an arrowhead still embedded in one of his vertebrae (to be seen in the Dorchester Museum). Following the barrage, the Roman infantry advanced up the slope, cutting its way from rampart to rampart until it reached the innermost bay, where some circular huts had recently been built. These were set alight, and under the rising clouds of smoke the gates were stormed and the position carried. But resistance had been obstinate and the fury of the legionaries was aroused. For a space, confusion, and massacre dominated the scene. Men and women, young and old, were savagely cut down before the troops were called to heel.
> A systematic slighting of the defences followed, whereafter the legion was withdrawn, doubtless taking hostages with it, and the dazed inhabitants were left to bury their dead amongst the ashes of the huts beside the gates. The task was carried out anxiously and without order, but, even so, from few graves were omitted those tributes of food and drink which were the proper requisites of the dead. With their cups and food-vessels and trinkets, the bones, often two or more skeletons huddled into a single grave and many of the skulls deeply scored with sword cuts, made a sad and dramatic showing – the earliest British war-cemetery known to us.

While today one might applaud the flair with which archaeologists wrote reports in those days, subsequent excavations have revealed that several assumptions Sir Mortimer Wheeler made to develop his 'Battle of the East Gate' theory cannot now be sustained. His assault theory rests on the presence of his 'war-cemetery', but he failed to show that of the 52 bodies discovered there, only 14 had died by violent means. Today archaeologists consider it more likely that the site was indeed a cemetery, but one which developed over time, and to which bodies were brought for burial. They were therefore not buried where they had fallen in defence of the eastern gateway. Modern forensic studies have even shown that some of those that sustained wounds did not die from them, but instead lived on for some time after receiving them.

Wheeler based his account of the burning of the fort's guard huts on his discovery of a charcoal layer just outside the eastern gateway. However, archaeologists now believe this was produced by iron-working, the evidence of which in the form of Celtic arrowheads now supports this theory rather than provides us with evidence of an assault. After all, bows were used in insignificant numbers by the Celts at this time, and their presence does not necessarily suggest that a unit of Celtic archers made a last stand on the spot. The only piece of evidence that has successfully stood the test of time is the slighting of the gateway – as revealed by the collapsed sides of the stone-clad gateway. The remains were overlaid by early Roman pottery, suggesting the collapse occurred prior to Roman settlement in the area – a date consistent with the Roman invasion. This is consistent with the idea of Vespasian's progress through southern England, and may represent a deliberate policy of destroying the gateways of Celtic fortifications as a means of guaranteeing the subjugation of the inhabitants.

Maiden Castle was not the only hill-fort attacked by the Romans, or even by the Celts. Around 100 BC the hill-fort of Danebury was destroyed, or at least its gateway was burned down. Tools and horse trappings were abandoned, suggesting a hurried departure of the inhabitants, or a violent end. The remains of 21 mutilated bodies were found in two grave pits close to the gate, of both sexes, and ranging in age from four to 45. The pits were never properly covered, suggesting open graves into which the bodies were thrown. All this points towards a violent end to the occupation of Danebury, but once again archaeology stops short of explaining what exactly happened. Professor Barry Cunliffe, the director of the Danebury excavation, suggested that the end of the fort was a result of tension created by a population expansion in southern England, but the full story may never be known.

At Hod Hill, Dorset there is evidence of the hurried repair and improvement of the defensive works, possibly undertaken as a response to news of the Roman invasion. The last-minute improvements did little to help the defenders, as there is evidence that Hod Hill was attacked by the Roman army in AD 43, almost certainly the work of Vespasian and his II (Augusta) Legion as it marched west through modern-day Dorset. The site was excavated during the 1950s by Sir Ian Richmond, who was particularly keen to find evidence of a Roman assault. What he did discover was even more intriguing. One of the roundhouses within the enclosure was larger than those around it, which might suggest it was the home of a chieftain or an important administrative building. Archaeologists uncovered 11 Roman ballista bolts amid its ruins, buried nose-first as if fired from the same location somewhere outside the south-east corner of the fort. The accuracy of the fire was particularly impressive, as the bolts were concentrated around that one target. It has been suggested that when the defenders of Hod Hill refused to surrender, the Romans demonstrated the efficiency of their siege train by destroying this one hut – thus prompting the garrison to open their gates. As there is no other evidence of battle this remains a plausible explanation of what happened, but as usual the evidence is open to interpretation. Certainly Vespasian considered the site to be important: he ordered the building of a Roman auxiliary camp in the north-east corner of the Iron Age defences.

Another site worth noting is that of Burnswark in Dumfries, a hill-fort flanked by the remains of two Roman siege camps. When the site was first excavated in 1898 it was assumed that Burnswark had been besieged by the Romans, whose camps were built within siege-engine range of the ramparts. However, more recent excavations conducted in the 1970s have proved that the Roman siegeworks were

Clickhimin in Shetland is another broch settlement, built in various stages between 200 and 50 BC. The entrance to the broch itself was protected by this 'blockhouse', and an outlying circular stone rampart enclosed the surrounding settlement. (Historic Scotland)

50

Dun Telve is one of two Iron Age brochs built in Glen Elg, Rossshire, close to the Isle of Skye (its partner being Dun Troddan). It is the largest surviving broch structure to be found on the Scottish mainland, with its remaining section of wall extending to a height of just over 10m. (Stratford Archive)

built after the fort fell into disuse, almost certainly providing a training ground for the Roman troops stationed in southern Scotland during the late 1st century and early 2nd century AD. In effect the hill-fort had become a Roman firing range. This suggests that the Romans took the reduction of hill-forts seriously, possibly as a means of preparing for campaigns against the un-pacified Celtic tribes to the north. These works are in stark contrast to the lack of Roman siegeworks in the rest of Britain, which suggests that if the Romans ever encountered a fortress that defied them, they would lay siege to it in accordance with their military doctrine, establishing secure camps from which to bombard the defences. Once the defenders were driven from the ramparts the Romans would probably send in auxiliary troops to secure the fort, holding their veteran legionaries back as a reserve.

This is how the Romans fought at Mons Graupius (AD 84) against the Caledonii, or when they pacified Gaul, Judaea and Dacia. The lack of fortified camps in the British Isles suggests that instances of resistance against the Romans were rare. It is more likely that the methods suggested at Hod Hill – a demonstration of Roman military might – were sufficient to force the surrender of most of Britain's Celtic fortresses. While it is appealing to imagine the defence of sites such as Maiden Castle as romantic last stands by the Celtic inhabitants in Britain, the truth was probably much more mundane. Faced with the futility of resistance, the defenders made peace with the invaders, so bringing the era of their political and military independence to a close.

Aftermath

The Roman invasion of Britain in AD 43 sounded the death knell for Celtic culture in southern Britain. We have already seen how hill-forts like Maiden Castle continued to be used for two or even three decades afterwards, before they were replaced by a Roman provincial town a few miles away. In the case of Maiden Castle there is evidence that the population began to drift away from the old fortified settlement during this period, so that in the space of one or two generations the population dwindled away until only a few inhabitants remained. The Romans brought peace in their wake (if we ignore the Iceni revolt of AD 61–63), and therefore the British population had less need to protect themselves and their communities. The Roman policy of slighting the defences of the hill-forts that submitted to them or were captured made these places indefensible, and speeded the drift towards new settlements. However, the process of pacification was not completely smooth. Archaeologists have shown that the gateway of the hill-fort of South Cadbury in Somerset was destroyed around AD 70–80, which suggests the fort remained occupied after AD 43, but that it was probably attacked and destroyed by the Romans in what might well have been a punitive and retaliatory action. It appears that the fort was then completely abandoned until the Roman occupation of southern Britain came to an end around AD 410.

The pattern appears fairly clear. In areas where the Romans brought the population directly under their control the old fortifications fell into disuse – if not immediately, then within less than three generations. In the north and west of what is now England, where the Romanization of the population was less thorough, the occupation of some forts continued for many decades, and in some cases throughout the Roman period. Unfortunately we know all too little about this period of occupancy, including whether these sites retained their older levels of population and sense of community, or if their population declined almost as dramatically as that of the hill-fort dwellers of southern England. Some hill-forts were certainly either abandoned or else changed their role from fortified settlements into fortified farmsteads, with a consequent drop in population. The process of Roman expansion was a gradual one, as Agricola only pushed into what is now southern Scotland in AD 82–83. By then the strongholds of the Brigantes of today's northern England had fallen under Roman control, so the Celts of Scotland and Wales remained the only truly independent indigenous tribes in the British Isles.

The eastern gateway defences of Maiden Castle, photographed during Sir Mortimer Wheeler's excavation there in 1935. The sheer scale of the banks would make any assault a difficult proposition for an Iron Age force, although the defences would present less difficulty to a Roman engineer. (The Society of Antiquaries, London)

We know from archaeology that many of the more important hill-forts in both southern Scotland and Wales remained in use during the period of Roman occupation, evidence that is supported by the historical record. These tribes became Roman 'clients', and while allowed to govern themselves, they became 'Romanized', losing their military and economic freedom in the process. Hill-forts such as Traprain Law in East Lothian became an important regional centre again after the Romans departed, as the capital of the Goddodin tribe – the new power in post-Roman southern Scotland. The situation in Wales was similar. As the region became a Roman military garrison rather than a fully integrated part of Roman Britain, there was less incentive for the indigenous population to abandon their old ways – or their old fortified settlements. Although Roman punitive expeditions ensured that the tribesmen of the Welsh mountains were not considered a threat, for the most part these people managed to retain a greater degree of independence than their Celtic neighbours to the east. Consequently hill-forts such as Tre'r Ceiri remained in continuous occupation during the Roman period.

During his 1935 excavation Sir Mortimer Wheeler examined the composition of the defensive inner rampart of Maiden Castle, and discovered it was constructed using chalk rubble and stone, overlaid with earth. The rampart was then topped by a wooden palisade. (The Society of Antiquaries, London)

In Wales and southern Scotland a handful of hill-forts were pressed into service by the Romans, who used them as military training grounds. At Caer-y-Twr in Anglesey a section of wall was demolished, and it has been suggested that this was done by the Romans as part of a training exercise – practising for a punitive expedition, as the attack on South Cadbury might have been. We have already mentioned how the hill-fort of Burnswark in Dumfriesshire was flanked by two Roman camps, both of which boasted a series of pits designed for siege engines lining the forward edge of the Roman siege line. Slingshot stones made from baked clay were also found on the site, suggesting the Romans practised their siege techniques against the abandoned hill-fort, but manned the defences with their own auxiliaries to heighten the realism of the exercise. Then there is the

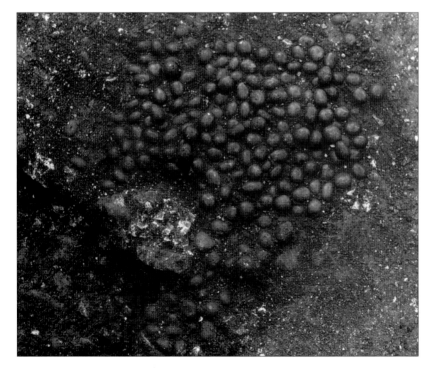

Among the artefacts discovered at Maiden Castle during the 1986 excavation were small caches of stones – presumably used as ammunition for Celtic slingshots. These would have been the primary form of defensive firepower available to the Ancient British defenders of hill-forts in the south of England during the period of the Roman invasion. (English Heritage)

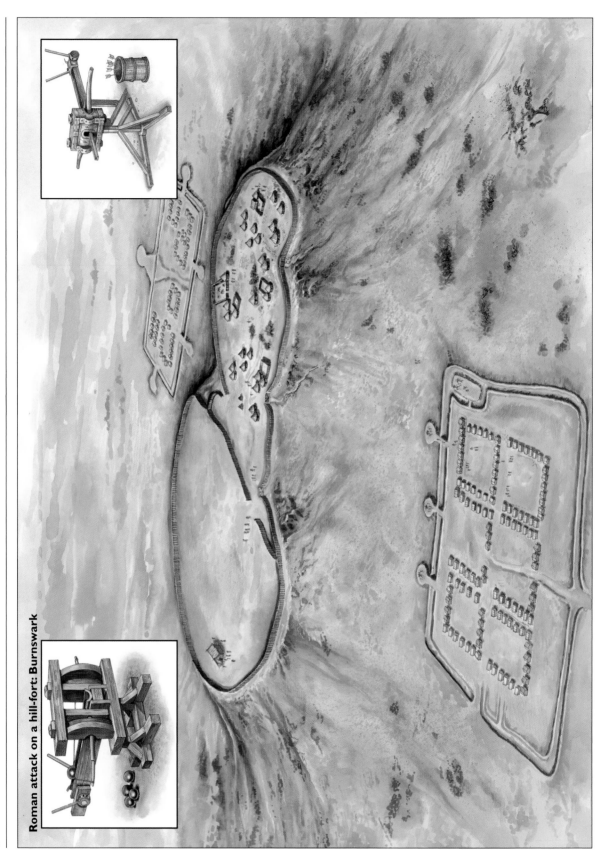

Roman attack on a hill-fort: Burnswark

LEFT **Roman attack on a hill-fort: Burnswark**
The evidence for a Roman assault on a hill-fort is scant, although archaeological finds at both Maiden Castle and Hod Hill in southern England both suggest that the defenders attempted to resist the Romans. Burnswark in southern Scotland is unique in that the Romans built two military encampments on either side of the small hill-fort, complete with artillery positions for Roman siege engines. However, the archaeological evidence suggests that the hill-fort was abandoned before the Roman camps were built. It is now supposed that these Roman works were training camps, where the Roman garrison in Scotland could practise siege techniques. They would then employ these skills during one of several punitive Roman expeditions into northern Scotland, or when called upon to quell a revolt further south. The hill-fort defences were designed around the slingshot – the standard defensive missile weapon of Ancient Britain. At Burnswark caches of clay slingshot stones were found – akin to modern dummy bullets. This suggests the Romans used auxiliaries to represent Celtic defenders during their mock attacks on Burnswark fort. Also shown are two types of Roman ballista (top left and right).

example of Hod Hill, where a Roman fort was built into one corner of the old Iron Age earthworks. While this was probably a matter of prime location and economy of effort, it certainly appears that the Romans were aware of the threat posed by the occupancy of hill-forts by hostile tribesmen or rebels, and trained themselves to deal with just such a situation.

Finally we have already seen how some hill-forts such as Danebury in Hampshire served as religious as well as political centres. It is therefore not completely surprising that after its fall Danebury remained in use during the Roman period, as evidenced by cartwheel tracks and Romanized finds discovered on top of the older layers of occupancy and defence. It has been suggested that the fort housed a small religious community, which remained in residence to maintain the sanctity of a sacred site. A similar site may well have existed in Maiden Castle, as the older Romano-British Christian temple built there might well have been placed on the site of an older place of worship.

These Iron Age hill-forts came into their own again after the Romans left Britain. During the 5th and 6th centuries AD several were re-occupied, as the defenceless towns of Sub-Roman Britain were vulnerable to attack by a growing number of invaders. However, it appears that the people of Sub-Roman Britain appeared well aware of the defensive possibilities of sites such as South Cadbury and Castle Dore, both of which were re-fortified during what is sometimes known as the 'Arthurian' period. In less Romanized areas, forts such as Dinas Emrys in Wales and Dun Eidin (Edinburgh) or Traprain Law in Scotland became important political centres once again – which must be left for another study.

Not far from the hill-fort of Lordenshaws, Northumberland is this stone, containing a series of 'cup and ring' marks. Cup marks carved into boulders and other stones are believed to date to the Bronze Age, although no satisfactory explanation has so far been given as to their purpose. However, one 19th-century antiquarian suggested these marks represented a relief map of local hill-forts. Their proximity to several fortified sites suggests that these locations were of local importance long before any fortification was built there. (Courtesy of Keith Durham)

The sites today

The following selection of Iron Age Celtic fortifications includes sites owned and maintained by national bodies such as English Heritage, Scottish Heritage or Welsh Heritage, or by local authorities such as Hampshire County Council. Almost all of the sites listed are open to the public, and some form of self-guided tour is available to visitors. A few others have been included because the sites are highly visible, even though direct access to them is sometimes restricted, often because the site is no longer in good repair. Some sites are even supported by a museum either at the site or in a nearby town, where artefacts recovered from the excavation of the site are now displayed.

Finally a handful of national or major regional museums are included in the following list, as they contain artefacts which have either been recovered from the sites of Iron Age fortifications mentioned in this book, or which help expand our understanding of the people who built these defensive works. Where appropriate website links have been included.

As this book has limited itself to a discussion of Celtic fortifications found on the mainland of Britain or the Scottish islands, sites and museums in both the Republic of Ireland and Northern Ireland have been omitted. There are hundreds of Iron Age fortified sites throughout Britain, so only a handful of these can be included in the following list. For a more detailed gazetteer of hill-forts in Britain, readers are directed to A.H.A. Hogg's *Hill-forts of Britain* (1975), a work that includes a detailed if somewhat dated survey of all known sites.

Scotland
Fortified sites

The Broch of Mousa, Shetland
The finest surviving broch structure, standing over 13m high. Owned by Scottish Heritage. Located on the island of Mousa, accessible by ferry boat from Sandwick, 14 miles south of Lerwick, Shetland. See the Historic Scotland website (*www.historic-scotland.gov.uk*) for ferry information and opening times. Alternatively call the Historic Scotland office in Skara Brae, Orkney for up-to-date information: (01856) 841815.

Clickhimin Broch, Shetland
Broch tower and associated settlement and outer defences. Owned by Scottish Heritage. Located one mile south-west of Lerwick, Shetland. See the Visit Shetland website (*www.visitshetland.com*) for opening times and contact information.

Hambledon Hill, Dorset was built in two phases on a narrow, winding ridge, the oldest portion of the site being on the northern end of the ridge – to the right of this view. In its final form the hill-fort enclosed an area of approximately 10 hectares. (RCAHM)

The impressive Iron Age hill-fort at Yarnbury in Wiltshire was built around an earlier fort during the 1st century BC, and has been associated with the Belgae. The distinctive ravelin in front of the gateway probably acted as a miniature fort in its own right. (RCAHM)

The Broch of Gurness, Orkney

A superbly situated Iron Age broch and fortified village. The site also contains a small museum. Owned by Scottish Heritage. Located 15 miles north-west of Kirkwall, Orkney. Open in the summer season only (1 April to 30 September) For further information call (01856) 751414 or visit the Historic Scotland website listed above.

The Broch of Midhowe, Orkney

A well-preserved seashore broch and settlement. Owned by Scottish Heritage. Located on the island of Rousay. Accessible by ferry from Tingwall, on the Orkney mainland. Call (01856) 751360 for ferry details, and (01856) 841815 for access information and opening times, or visit the Historic Scotland website listed above.

Dun Carloway Broch, Lewis

A broch perched above Loch Roag on the western coast of Lewis. Owned by the Doune Broch Centre. Open in the summer season only (1 April to 30 September). Visitor centre and museum adjacent to the site. For further information call (01851) 643338, or see *www.undiscoveredscotland.co.uk/lewis/duncarloway/index.html* and *www.themodernantiquarian.com/site/791*.

Dun Telve, Glenelg

One of two broch towers in Glenelg on the Scottish mainland near Skye, both standing over 10m high. Owned by Scottish Heritage. For visitor information call (01667) 460232.

Traprain Law, East Lothian

An impressive hill-fort, dominating the East Lothian coastal plain. Private ownership but public access permitted. Consult the following websites for detailed information on access to the site: *www.cyberscotia.com/ancient-lothian/index.html* and *www.themodernantiquarian.com/site/607*.

White Caterthun and Brown Caterthun, Angus

Located near Brechin, Angus within sight of each other, the hill-forts of White Caterthun and Brown Caterthun are in private hands, but accessible to the public. See the following websites for further information: *www.themodernantiquarian.com/site/3031, www.stonepages.com/scotland/ bwcaterthun.html* and *www.undiscoveredscotland.co.uk/bridgend/caterthuns*.

Eildon Hill North, Scottish Borders

Located near Melrose in the Scottish Borders. In private hands but accessible to the public. See the following website for more information: *www.discovertheborders.co.uk/places/202.html*.

Woden Law, Scottish Borders

Located near Hownam in the Scottish Borders. In private hands but accessible to the public. See the following website for more information: *www.megalithic.co.uk/article.php?sid=10649*.

Burnswark, Dumfries & Galloway

An Iron Age hill-fort that was used by the Romans as a military training ground. In private hands but accessible to the public. See the following websites for more information: *www.roman-britain.org/places/burnswark.htm* and *www.themodernantiquarian.com/site/6412*.

Museums

The Orkney Museum, Tankerness House, Kirkwall, Orkney
An excellent collection of Iron Age artefacts, as well as a detailed introduction to prehistoric Orkney. For details call (01856) 773191, or visit the museum website: *www.orkneyheritage.com*.

Shetland Museum, Lower Hillhead, Lerwick, Shetland
A fascinating collection of archaeological artefacts relating to Shetland's Iron Age past. For details call (01595) 695057, or visit the museum website: *www.shetland-museum.org.uk/index.htm*.

National Museum of Scotland, Chamber Street, Edinburgh
Scotland's premier history museum, it contains numerous Iron Age artefacts, including objects and hoards recovered from Traprain Law and other fortified sites. Open daily from 10am to 5pm. For further information visit the museum website: *www.nms.ac.uk/scotland/home/index.asp*.

Oakbank Crannog, Kenmore, Loch Tay, Perthshire
A reconstruction of an Iron Age loch dwelling (or 'crannog'), the structure is based on the archaeological investigation of the original crannog located on the opposite bank of Loch Tay. The Oakbank Crannog Centre site includes an exhibition that helps interpret the Iron Age landscape of the area, integrating crannogs with the hinterland, and even the ring forts guarding the area. The author participated in the underwater excavation of the original structure back in the mid-1980s. The Oakbank Crannog Centre is open from 15 March to 31 October. Call (01887) 830583 for further information, or visit their website: *http://www.crannog.co.uk/index.html*.

England
Fortified sites

Maiden Castle, near Dorchester, Dorset
The largest Iron Age hill-fort in Britain, the imposing fortifications of Maiden Castle were excavated during the 1930s and 1980s. The site is now maintained by English Heritage. Maiden Castle is open throughout the year, and a self-guided trail is provided. Website: *www.english-heritage.org.uk/server/show/ConProperty.279*.

Danebury, near Stockbridge, Hampshire
The Iron Age hill-fort of Danebury was extensively excavated over some 20 years, making it the most closely studied hill-fort site in Britain. Danebury is now maintained by Hampshire County Council. The site is open throughout the year, and a self-guided trail is provided. Website: *www.hants.gov.uk /countryside /danebury/index.html*.

Stanwick, near Forcett, North Yorkshire
Excavated by Sir Mortimer Wheeler in the early 1950s, Stanwick was the Late Iron age capital of the Brigantes, the most important tribe in pre-Roman northern Britain. The oldest section of the 310-hectare site is now maintained by English Heritage. The site is open throughout the year, and a self-guided trail is provided. Website: *www.english-heritage.org.uk/server/show/ onProperty.384*.

Old Sarum, near Winchester, Hampshire
The Iron Age hill-fort at Old Sarum (the original site of the town of Winchester) remained in near-constant use until the 12th century, and became the

Hod Hill in Dorset is unique in that the Romans built an auxiliary fort in the north-west quadrant of the Iron Age fortification. The hill-fort was first built around 400 BC, but was modified extensively until the Roman invasion. The presence of iron bolts from Roman siege engines confirms Roman reports that the hill-fort was stormed and captured by the II Legion in AD 43. (RCAHM)

The hill-fort at Winklebury, Wiltshire was built in three phases, the earliest being the staggered barrier stretching across the steep-sided ridge (in the background of this view). The defences were then extended around the edge of the slope during the 3rd century BC. Finally in the mid-1st century BC the defences were consolidated into the smaller, oval-shaped hill-fort seen in the foreground. (RCAHM)

site of a Norman castle. The site is now maintained by English Heritage. Old Sarum is open throughout the year, and a self-guided trail is provided. Website: *www.english-heritage.org.uk/server/show/ConProperty.293.*

Blackbury Camp, near Honiton, Devon
Sitting astride a narrow ridge, the Iron Age hill-fort at Blackbury Camp (also known as Blackbury Castle) was excavated during the 1950s, when the site's unusual entrance was examined in detail. The site is now maintained by English Heritage. Blackbury Camp is open throughout the year, and a self-guided trail is provided. Website: *www.english-heritage.org.uk/server/show/ ConProperty.239.*

Bratton Camp, near Westbury, Wiltshire
The well-preserved Iron Age hill-fort at Bratton Camp was built beside an older Neolithic barrow, and shares its hill with a white horse carved into the chalk slopes. The site is now maintained by English Heritage. Bratton is open throughout the year, and a self-guided trail is provided. Website: *www.english-heritage.org.uk /server/show/ConProperty.242.*

Old Oswestry, Oswestry, Shropshire
A large and complex hill-fort situated a mile from the modern town of Oswestry, on the Welsh borders. The site is now maintained by English Heritage. It is open throughout the year, and a self-guided trail is provided. Website: *www.english-heritage.org.uk/server/show/ConProperty.349.*

The hill-fort of Pen Dinas overlooking Aberystwyth in Cardigan was excavated in the 1930s, when it was revealed the fort was built in three phases, the final one being completed during the 1st century AD, and encompassing both hills on the same ridge. (RCAHM)

Uffington Castle, near Wantage, Oxfordshire

The hill-fort at Uffington dominated the 'Ridgeway', an ancient upland track that crossed central and southern England during the Bronze Age and Iron Age. The Bronze Age white horse carved into an adjacent hillside is the largest and oldest carving of this type in Britain, while a series of nearby burial mounds also predate the hill-fort, and attest to Uffington's prehistoric importance. The site is now maintained by English Heritage. Uffington Castle is open throughout the year, and a self-guided trail is provided. Website: *www.englishheritage.org.uk/server/show/ConProperty.224*.

Museums

The British Museum, Russell Street, London

The premier history museum in Britain, the British Museum contains a vast collection of Iron Age artefacts. The museum boasts one of the best archaeological bookshops in the world. Nearest underground stations are Holborn or Russell Square. For opening times and further information contact the museum on (0207) 323 8299, or visit their website at *www.thebritishmuseum.ac.uk*.

Dorset County Museum, High West Street, Dorchester, Dorset

A superb archaeological collection, including artefacts relating to Maiden Castle and other Iron Age hill-forts in the area. Contact the museum on (01305) 262735 or visit their website for further information and opening times: *www.dorsetcountymuseum.org/index.htm*.

Hull and East Riding Museum, High Street, Hull

The collection contains an Iron Age logboat and other artefacts relating to the Iron Age in northern England. Contact the museum on (01482) 300300. No dedicated website at present.

Butser Ancient Farm, Horndean, Waterlooville, Hampshire

A reconstruction of an Iron Age village. Generally open at weekends only. For details contact the farm on (01239) 891319, or visit their website: *www.butser.org.uk*.

Flag Fen, The Droveway, Northey Road, Peterborough

A reconstructed Late Bronze Age settlement, complete with a working farm. The waterlogged timbers of the original lake-dwelling settlement are still in situ, and can be viewed by visitors. The site also contains the reconstruction of an Iron Age roundhouse. The Flag Fen site is open all year. Call (01733) 313414 for information, or visit their website: *www.flagfen.com*.

Museum of the Iron Age, 6 Church Close, Andover, Hampshire

The museum is the only one in Britain dedicated to the interpretation of an Iron Age hill-fort, in this case Danebury. The museum contains reconstructions and models of the fort as well as artefacts recovered during its excavation. Open throughout the year from Tuesdays to Saturdays. For further information call (01264) 366283, or visit their website: *www.hants.gov.uk/museum/ironagem*.

Peat Moors Centre, Shapwick Road, Westhay, Somerset

A fascinating prehistoric interpretation centre on the outskirts of Glastonbury, the site includes a series of reconstructions, including Iron Age roundhouses based on those found at the Glastonbury lake village, and an inter-pretation of the prehistoric trackways known as the 'Somerset Levels' which once crossed the boggy area around the site. Open from 1 April until 31 October, daily (except Wednesdays). For further information call (01458) 860697, or visit their website: *www.somerset.gov.uk/somerset/cultureheritage/heritage/pmc*.

Wales

Fortified sites

Tre'r Ceiri, Llyn Peninsula, Gwynedd
A spectacular stone-built hill-fort. Full public access via footpaths. Website: *www.penllyn.com/1/gallery/llithfaen/5.html*.

Dinas Emrys, Ffestiniog, Gwynedd
A small hill-fort, with stong post-Roman links. Private ownership, but access available by permission from local farmer. Website: *www.vortigernstudies.org.uk /artcit/dinas.htm*.

Caer-y-Twr, near Holyhead, Anglesey
A small but important hill-fort, in private ownership but accessible to the public via footpaths leading up Holyhead mountain from the town. Website: *www.megalithic.co.uk/article.php?sid=5955*.

Pen Dinas, Aberystwyth, Ceredig
A hill-fort overlooking the modern town of Aberystwyth. Public access. Website: *www.walespast.com/article.shtml?id=41*.

Castell Henllys, Meline, Crymych, Pembrokeshire
A partially reconstructed Iron Age hill-fort with reconstructed roundhouses. Owned by the Pembroke Coast National Park. Shop and small interpretation centre on site. Call (01239) 891319 for details. Website: *www.castellhenllys.com*.

Museums

The National Museum of Wales, Cathays Park, Cardiff
The museum displays cover the Iron Age in Wales, and the collection includes artefacts recovered from hill-forts. Open daily (except Mondays) from 10am to 5pm. For further information visit the museum website: *www.museumwales.ac.uk/en/home*.

Warham hill-fort in Norfolk was protected by two substantial circular ramparts separated by a ditch, although the position of the original gateway is unclear. The banks encompassed a 1.4 hectare enclosure. (RCAHM)

Bibliography

Armit, Ian *Towers in the North: The Brochs of Scotland* (Stroud, Gloucestershire: Tempus Publishing, 2003)

Armit, Ian *Celtic Scotland* (London: B.T. Batsford for Historic Scotland, 2005)

Barrett, J.C. *et al.*, *Cadbury Castle, Somerset* (London: B.T. Batsford for English Heritage, 2001)

Bradley, R. and Ellison, A. *Rams Hill – British Archaeological Reports No. 19* (Oxford: Archaeopress, 1975)

Chadwick, Nora and Cunliffe, Barry *The Celts: A Penguin History* (London: Penguin, 1997)

Cunliffe, Barry and Miles, David *Aspects of the Iron Age in Central South Britain* (Oxford: Oxford University School of Archaeology, 1984)

Cunliffe, Barry *Iron Age Communities in Britain* (London: Routledge, 1991; 3rd edition)

Cunliffe, Barry *Danebury* (London: B.T. Batsford for English Heritage, 1993)

Cunliffe, Barry *Iron Age Britain* (London: B.T. Batsford, 1995)

Cunliffe, Barry *The Ancient Celts* (Oxford: Oxford University Press, 1997)

Cunliffe, Barry *Facing the Ocean: The Atlantic and its Peoples, 8000 BC to AD 1500* (Oxford: Oxford University Press, 2004)

Cunliffe, Barry *Iron Age Communities in Britain: An Account of England, Scotland and Wales from the Seventh Century BC until the Roman Conquest* (London: Routledge, 2004)

Dyer, James *Penguin Guide to Prehistoric England and Wales* (London: Penguin, 1981)

Dyer, James *Hillforts of England and Wales* (Risborough, Buckinghamshire: Shire Publications, 2003)

Fojut, Nopel *The Brochs of Gurness and Midhowe* (Edinburgh: Historic Scotland, 2001)

Forde-Johnston, James *Hillforts of the Iron Age in England and Wales: A Survey of the Surface Evidence* (Liverpool: University of Liverpool, 1976)

Guilbert, G. (ed.) *Hill-fort Studies* (Leicester: Leicester University Press, 1981)

Harding, D.W. *The Iron Age in the Upper Thames Basin* (Oxford: Oxford University Press, 1972)

Harding, D.W. (ed.) *Hillforts: Later Prehistoric Earthworks in Britain and Ireland* (London: Academic Press, 1976)

Harding, D.W. *Celts in Conflict: Hillfort Studies, 1922–77* (Edinburgh, University of Edinburgh, 1979)

Hawkes, Jacquetta *A Guide to the Prehistoric and Roman Monuments in England and Wales* (London: Chatto & Windus, 1951)

Hogg, A.H.A. *Hill-forts of Britain* (London: Hart-Davis, MacGibbon, 1975)

Hogg, A.H.A. *British Hill-Forts: An Index – British Archaeological Reports No. 62* (London, Archaeopress, 1979)

James, Simon *Uncovering the World of the Celts* (London: Thames & Hudson, 2005)

James, Simon and Rigby, Valerie *Britain and the Celtic Iron Age* (London: British Museum Press, 1997)

Konstam, Angus *Historic Atlas of the Celtic World* (New York: Facts on File, 2001)

Musson, Chris *The Breidden Hillfort: A Later Prehistoric Settlement* (London: Council for British Archaeology, 1991)

Pryor, Francis *Britain BC: Life in Britain and Ireland before the Romans* (London: Harper Perennial, 2003)

Ritchie, Anna and Graham *Scotland: Archaeology and Early History* (Edinburgh: Edinburgh University Press, 1981)

Ritchie, J.N.G. *The Brochs of Scotland* (Aylesbury, Buckinghamshire: Shire Publications, 1988)

Sharples, Niall M. *Maiden Castle* (London: B.T. Batsford for English Heritage, 1991)

Sharples, Niall M. *Scalloway: A Broch, Late Iron Age Settlement and Medieval Cemetery in Shetland – Oxbow Monographs on Archaeology* (London: Oxbow Books, 1998)

Wainwright, Richard *A Guide to Prehistoric Remains in Britain* (London, Constable, 1978)

Wheeler, (Sir) Mortimer *Maiden Castle, Dorset: Official Guidebook* (London: Her Majesty's Stationery Office – Department of the Environment, Ancient Monuments and Historic Buildings, 1972)

Glossary

Annex An extension to the earthworks of an Iron Age fort, often built as a later addition to the fortification system.

Bank In terms of hill-forts, these are often associated with ramparts, although more accurately the latter represents the final bank before the inner enclosure. Banks were usually but not always built behind a ditch, from which the soil for the bank was excavated.

Berm A flat space between the foot of a bank and the start of a ditch.

Bivallate An Iron Age fortification system where the central enclosure is surrounded by two sets of banks and associated ditches.

Bronze Age The period from around 2100 BC until 700 BC when bronze was produced by the indigenous peoples of Britain.

Compact A bivallate, trivallate or multivallate hill-fort where the systems of banks and ditches are close together – usually within 10m of each other.

Contour fort The technical term for a hill-fort built to take advantage of the contours of a hill. Invariably the shape of the fort follows the contour line, producing an irregular shape to the fortification.

Counterscarp The exterior slope or wall of a ditch, which in the case of hill-forts was sometimes revetted using stone or timber.

Dispersed A bivallate, trivallate or multivallate hill-fort where the systems of banks and ditches are well spaced out – usually more than 10m from each other.

Earthwork An earthen embankment, part of a fortification. In most cases a bank or rampart is classified as an earthwork.

Glacis The slope extending down from the outer works of a fortification over which an attacker would have to move as he approached the fort.

Hill-fort A defensive earthwork or stone-built Iron Age structure built on an easily defensible position, usually the plateau or summit of a hill.

Iron Age The period from around 700 BC until the Roman conquest of Britain in 43 AD when the inhabitants of Britain produced and used iron.

Multiple enclosure fort A form of earthwork or fortification where the defences form a network of banks and sometimes ditches. In terms of Iron Age fortifications it is generally presumed that these sites were non-military in nature, and the multiple enclosures contained within its defences were probably used to house farm buildings or livestock.

Multivallate An Iron Age fortification system where the central enclosure is surrounded by more than three sets of banks and associated ditches.

Neolithic The period between around 4200 BC and 2100 BC in Britain during which the indigenous peoples of Britain built standing stone monuments, and buried their prestigious dead in barrows or burial mounds.

Oppidum A Roman term for a fortified town or large settlement, usually associated with a hill-top position.

Palisade A wooden fence of stakes, posts and beams that formed a defensive barrier. In most cases these surmounted the ramparts of an Iron Age fort.

Plateau fort An Iron Age fortification built on flat or sloping ground, where there was no natural advantage of terrain that could augment the defensive qualities of the site. The fort had to rely on its man-made defences for protection.

Promontory fort An Iron Age fortification built on a headland or promontory, where three sides of the position were protected by the sea or even by rivers, leaving just one side which required protection from man-made defensive works.

Rampart In terms of hill-forts and other Iron Age fortifications, a rampart was the last bank defence before the inner enclosure of the fort. A rampart was often surmounted by a palisade, breastwork or other form of parapet.

Revetment A timber or stone facing to a bank, ditch counterscarp or rampart, designed to protect it from erosion, or to impart additional strength to the structure.

Timber-laced The archaeological term for a bank or rampart of earth or stone that was constructed around a timber frame.

Trivallate An Iron Age fortification system where the central enclosure is surrounded by three sets of banks and associated ditches.

Univallate An Iron Age fortification system where the central enclosure is surrounded by just one set of banks and associated ditches.

Vitrified The term applied to a stone-built Iron Age fortification where the stones were heated until they completely or partially fused together. This process imparted greater strength to the finished structure.

Index